BOBBY GALLAGHER

It's Not Unusual

Unoffiicial Fan Guide to Sir Tom Jones

First edition

This book was professionally typeset on Reedsy. Find out more at reedsy.com

Contents

1

A Warm Welcome

Hello there, fellow fans! Whether you're a die-hard Tom Jones aficionado who's been grooving to his tunes since the 1960s or a new fan who just discovered the soulful magic of "Delilah" on your favorite playlist, welcome to this celebration of one of music's greatest legends. If you're here, it means you've been touched by that unmistakable voice— yes, the one that could melt hearts, set the dance floor on fire, or, let's be honest, make a crowd lose their minds and throw their knickers on stage!

This book is a love letter to Sir Tom Jones, the Welsh wonder who took the world by storm and has kept us all tapping our feet, shedding a tear, or belting out his hits in the shower for over six decades. We'll be taking a deep dive into his extraordinary career, exploring the stories behind his music, his life behind the scenes, and his enduring legacy as a style icon, sex symbol, and, above all, a true artist. So grab a drink (maybe a glass of something Welsh?) and settle in for a celebration of the one and only Sir Tom.

Why We're Here: Celebrating the Legend

Tom Jones is not just a name; it's an institution. He's "The Voice" long before TV talent shows came up with that title. Whether he's crooning about heartbreak in "Without Love" or urging us to get up and dance with "Sex Bomb," Tom has a knack for capturing the essence of human emotions in a way that makes us feel like he's singing directly to us. And let's not forget those iconic hip shakes—seriously, he's the reason *hips don't lie.*

What makes Tom Jones so special? For starters, it's not just his music (although let's be real, those songs can take us to places we didn't know existed). It's the man behind the music— a man who's stayed true to himself, never afraid to adapt but always keeping his distinct voice and charm. Whether he's rocking a velvet suit in his Vegas days or sporting a crisp, tailored look in his modern performances, Tom's style, like his voice, is timeless.

So why write this book? Because, dear readers, Tom Jones deserves to be celebrated, honored, and—most importantly— remembered not just for the legendary hits we love but for his incredible journey from a coal miner's son in Pontypridd, Wales, to a global superstar. It's time to shine a light on the moments that made him the icon he is today, both on and off the stage.

The Magic of Tom Jones: An Overview

This book is more than just a timeline of Sir Tom's career; it's a backstage pass to the life of the man who taught us it's okay to be bold, to have fun, and to never, ever take yourself too seriously. Along the way, we'll uncover stories that will surprise even the most devoted fans. Did you know that *What's New Pussycat?* almost didn't make it to the recording studio because it was considered too outrageous? Or that Tom was once considered the "bad boy" of the music industry before it was cool to be one?

Tom's ability to reinvent himself through the years is nothing short of spectacular. From the soulful ballads of the '60s to the disco vibes of the '70s, and even dabbling in rock and electronic music in the '90s and beyond, Tom Jones has never been afraid to try something new. Like a true "Thunderball," he strikes just when we least expect it. He's a musical chameleon, but with one constant: that powerful, rich baritone voice that can make even the most mundane lyrics sound like a declaration of love (or heartbreak, depending on the mood).

Let's not forget that Tom Jones isn't just a singer; he's an entertainer. His performances are legendary, not just for the incredible vocals but for the showmanship that makes every concert feel like an event you simply *can't* miss. Whether it's belting out "Green, Green Grass of Home" in front of adoring fans or shaking things up with a cover of Prince's "Kiss," Tom brings his A-game every time. And, yes, he's probably the only man who can pull off a tight leather suit in his 70s and still make us swoon.

3

A Man for All Generations

One of the most remarkable things about Tom Jones is that he's transcended generations. In a world where artists often fade after a hit or two, Tom has remained a powerhouse in the music industry for over sixty years. *Sixty years*! That's more than enough time to go through a few fashion trends, musical phases, and, let's be honest, hairstyles. But Tom has done it all while staying true to who he is.

The question is: *How does he do it?* How does a singer who rose to fame in the era of The Beatles and Elvis Presley still manage to sell out arenas today? How does someone who's been knighted by the Queen (that's right, *Sir* Tom) still have the swagger to collaborate with younger artists like Wyclef Jean, Jack White, and Robbie Williams? The secret might just be that Tom Jones has never stopped loving what he does. And when you love something as much as he loves singing, it shows.

You see, Sir Tom doesn't just sing a song—he lives it, breathes it, makes it his own. Listening to him perform "I (Who Have Nothing)" feels like a soul-wrenching experience. When he sings "She's a Lady," you can practically hear the wink in his voice. It's this passion, this commitment to his craft, that has kept fans coming back for more, year after year.

The Man Behind the Music

Beyond the hits, beyond the stage lights and the screaming fans, there's another side to Tom Jones—one that's often hidden behind the charismatic smile and the powerhouse voice. He's a family man, who was married to his beloved Linda for nearly 60 years until her passing. Through all the highs and lows, Tom has always been the kind of person who remains grounded, a trait he attributes to his Welsh roots.

Tom's life is a story of resilience. From overcoming the struggles of his humble beginnings to dealing with the fickleness of fame, he's faced it all with a tenacity that's truly inspiring. And through it all, he's never lost that twinkle in his eye or that wicked sense of humor. After all, it's not unusual (sorry, couldn't resist) for Tom to crack a joke or two during his concerts—often at his own expense.

A Legacy That Lives On

As we take this journey together, let's remember that Tom Jones is more than just the songs the suits, or even the scandals. He's a testament to the power of talent, perseverance, and the courage to be different. In a world where trends come and go faster than you can say "Sex Bomb," Tom has remained a constant—someone we can always rely on to remind us that great music and a little bit of flair can brighten even the darkest days.

So, whether you're here because you love "It's Not Unusual" or because you're obsessed with his soulful rendition of "You Can Leave Your Hat On," this book is for you. It's for everyone who's ever sung along, danced to his hits, or just marveled at how one man can keep captivating us decade after decade.

Now, let's turn the page and dive into the world of Tom Jones—the legend, the voice, the *man*

2

From Pontypridd to Stardom

Childhood in Wales: Growing up in Pontypridd

Our story begins in a small, unassuming town nestled in the heart of Wales—Pontypridd. It was here, on a misty day in June 1940, that Thomas John Woodward was born into a modest working-class family. Tom's father, a coal miner, and his mother, a homemaker, could never have imagined that their son would one day become an international sensation known simply as Tom Jones.

Pontypridd in the 1940s was a place where hard work and resilience were part of the fabric of daily life. The coal mines provided both the town's livelihood and its challenges. Tom grew up in a close-knit community where neighbors knew one another, and music was often the centerpiece of social gatherings. He fondly recalls the sounds of Welsh choirs, traditional hymns, and the rich musical heritage that surrounded him. Little did anyone know, though, that the boy who loved to sing at local gatherings would soon take his voice far beyond the valleys of

Wales.

Early Influences and Love for Music

Even as a child, Tom Jones had an unmistakable gift—a voice that could stop you in your tracks. He began singing at an early age, performing for friends and family with the kind of passion that left no doubt he was destined for something special. But Tom's love for music wasn't limited to just Welsh hymns; he was equally fascinated by American rock 'n' roll, rhythm and blues, and soul. As a teenager, he would listen to artists like Little Richard, Elvis Presley, and Chuck Berry on the radio, dreaming of the day he could perform on stage like his idols.

Tom's early love for music wasn't just a hobby—it was his lifeline. At the age of 12, he contracted tuberculosis, a serious illness that forced him to be bedridden for nearly two years. But even during those tough times, his voice never left him. Singing in bed became his solace, a way to lift his spirits and keep his dreams alive. Tom later said that this period was a defining moment in his life; it was when he realized just how deeply music was a part of his soul.

The Journey from Local Gigs to His First Big Break

Once Tom recovered from his illness, there was no stopping him. By the late 1950s, he had married his high school sweetheart, Linda Trenchard, at just 16 years old. Tom became a young father and took on various jobs to make ends meet, but his love for music was relentless. By night, he was performing in local pubs and working men's clubs across South Wales. It was during these gigs that he honed his skills, developing the powerful, soulful voice that would soon captivate audiences far beyond the Welsh valleys.

In the early 1960s, Tom joined a local band called The Senators, performing covers of rock 'n' roll and rhythm and blues hits. His commanding stage presence and powerful vocals quickly earned him a reputation as the hottest act in town. But while The Senators gained popularity locally, they struggled to break into the broader music scene. It seemed as though Tom was destined to remain a local hero—until fate intervened.

Tom's big break came in 1964 when a London-based manager named Gordon Mills caught one of his performances in a smoky club. Mills was immediately struck by Tom's raw talent, charisma, and voice that could shake the rafters. He knew he had found a star. Mills took Tom under his wing, encouraging him to rebrand himself as "Tom Jones"—a name that was catchy, marketable, and aligned perfectly with the hit film *Tom Jones* that had recently won an Oscar.

The Birth of a Star

With Gordon Mills' guidance, Tom Jones recorded his first single, "Chills and Fever," in 1964. Although it didn't make much of a splash, it was his second single, "It's Not Unusual," that truly catapulted him to fame. The song, with its infectious rhythm and Tom's soulful, powerful vocals, became an instant hit. In 1965, "It's Not Unusual" shot to the top of the UK charts and even broke into the American market, landing in the Top 10 of the Billboard Hot 100.

Suddenly, the young boy from Pontypridd was a global star. Within a matter of months, Tom went from performing in small clubs to appearing on iconic shows like *Top of the Pops* and *The Ed Sullivan Show*. His dynamic performances, signature hip swivels, and undeniable stage presence made him an overnight sensation. Audiences were mesmerized—not just by his voice but by the sheer energy and passion he brought to every performance.

Tom's rise to fame was as rapid as it was extraordinary, but he never forgot where he came from. Throughout his career, he has spoken fondly of his Welsh roots, his humble beginnings, and the people who shaped him. Tom's journey from Pontypridd to the top of the charts is a testament to his talent, determination, and the power of dreams.

Looking Ahead

Tom Jones' story is one of resilience, talent, and sheer determination. From a young boy singing in the valleys of Wales to becoming an international icon, his journey is nothing short of remarkable. But this is only the beginning. As we explore the rest of his incredible career in the following chapters, we'll uncover how Tom continued to evolve, facing the ups and downs of fame while remaining true to himself.

So, as we turn the page, get ready to dive into the world of Tom Jones—a man whose voice, charm, and spirit continue to inspire fans around the world.

Becoming "Tom Jones"

Imagine this: It's 1964, and a young singer from Wales, with a voice as deep as the coal mines that surrounded his hometown, is trying to make a name for himself. But back then, he wasn't yet *Tom Jones*—he was still plain old Thomas John Woodward. Sure, he had that smooth baritone and undeniable stage presence, but something was missing. He needed that extra *je ne sais quoi* to transform him from just another pub crooner to the superstar we know today. And thus began the metamorphosis into the legendary Tom Jones.

A Star is (Re)born: The Creation of "Tom Jones"

Before Tom was *Sir Tom Jones*—before the knickers started flying on stage, and before he became the beloved voice behind classics like "She's a Lady" and "What's New Pussycat?"—he was simply Tommy Woodward, a boy with big dreams and a bigger voice. But let's be honest: "Tommy Woodward" doesn't exactly scream "international heartthrob," does it?

Enter Gordon Mills, a savvy manager with a vision. Mills was the fairy godfather Tom never knew he needed. He took one look at this raw talent from Pontypridd and knew he was destined for something bigger. The problem? The name just didn't have that *showbiz* flair. So, after a brainstorming session and perhaps a few too many cups of tea, Mills came up with the perfect solution:

Tom Jones. The name was inspired by the hit 1963 film *Tom Jones* starring Albert Finney, which had swept the Oscars that year. The name wasn't just catchy—it was sexy, timeless, and, crucially, easy to remember.

And just like that, Tom Jones was born—not in a hospital, but in the smoke-filled backroom of a London club. With a new name and a fresh image, Tommy Woodward from Wales was ready to take on the world.

The Breakthrough Single: "It's Not Unusual"

Every superstar has that one song that changes everything. For Tom, it was "It's Not Unusual." But let's rewind for a moment—because it almost didn't happen!

In the early days, Tom was still trying to find his sound. He'd done covers, he'd belted out rock 'n' roll hits, but he needed something original—something that would grab the world's attention. In walked Gordon Mills (again, the hero of our story) with a song that was initially meant for someone else. Yes, you heard that right! "It's Not Unusual" was originally offered to none other than Sandie Shaw, but fate (and a busy schedule) intervened. Shaw's loss was Tom's gain.

Tom recorded the demo, and as soon as the first few chords were laid down, there was an electricity in the air. His voice wrapped around those swinging brass notes like they were made for each other. The song was a delicious cocktail of pop, soul, and that unmistakable Tom Jones *oomph*. When the demo made its way to Decca Records, they knew they had a hit on their hands.

In early 1965, "It's Not Unusual" was released as a single, and the world was never the same. The song exploded onto the charts, hitting #1 in the UK and crossing the pond to become a Top 10 hit in the United States. Suddenly, the boy from Pontypridd was rubbing shoulders with The Beatles and The Rolling Stones. Not too shabby for a guy who used to sing in smoky Welsh pubs, right?

What made "It's Not Unusual" such a sensation? It was that infectious rhythm, those brass blasts, and, of course, Tom's powerhouse voice. But let's not forget those now-iconic hip shakes that sent audiences into a frenzy. Women swooned, men took notes, and suddenly, everyone wanted to know: *Who is this Tom Jones?*

Signing with Decca Records: The Rise to International Fame

With a hit single under his belt, Tom was riding high. But to really solidify his place in music history, he needed the backing of a major label. Enter Decca Records, the label known for discovering The Rolling Stones and other major acts. Decca was looking for the next big thing, and they found it in Tom Jones.

13

When Tom signed with Decca, it was like strapping a rocket to his career. The label saw his potential and was determined to turn him into a global star. With their support, Tom began to release hit after hit. Songs like "What's New Pussycat?" and "Thunderball" (yes, the James Bond theme!) cemented his place as one of the hottest names in the industry.

But fame didn't come without its challenges. Tom was suddenly in demand everywhere—from London to Las Vegas. He was performing on TV shows like *Top of the Pops* and *The Ed Sullivan Show*, dazzling audiences with that unmistakable voice and those charismatic moves. His schedule was grueling, but Tom was living his dream. After all, it's not every day that a coal miner's son from Wales gets to share the stage with the likes of Elvis Presley and Sammy Davis Jr.

Tom's newfound fame also came with its fair share of wild moments. During one particularly memorable performance, fans were so enamored that they started throwing their underwear onto the stage—a tradition that would follow him for decades. (Tom, ever the gentleman, took it all in stride. "It's Not Unusual" to have your fans show you *that* kind of affection, right?)

From Stardom to Superstardom: The Transformation

With his career in full swing, Tom Jones was unstoppable. By the late 1960s, he had conquered not just the music charts but also the hearts of millions. His voice was on every radio, his face on every magazine cover. But it wasn't just the music that fans loved—it was Tom himself. He had that rare combination of talent, charm, and a little bit of cheekiness that made him irresistible. He wasn't just a singer; he was an *entertainer*.

Tom's fashion sense also became iconic during this time. Whether it was the tailored suits, unbuttoned shirts, or that famous gold medallion, he had a style that was bold, brash, and completely his own. He was a man who could sing about heartbreak in "Without Love" one minute and then turn around and have the audience dancing with "Delilah" the next. And let's not forget those hip swivels—Tom's secret weapon that could make even the stiffest of crowds loosen up.

The Legacy Begins

By the time the 1970s rolled around, Tom Jones was no longer just a singer—he was a cultural phenomenon. He had gone from small-town boy to international superstar in just a few short years, all thanks to his undeniable talent, hard work, and a little bit of luck. But if you asked Tom, he'd say it was more than just luck. It was the power of believing in himself, staying true to his roots, and, most importantly, always giving it his all.

Looking back, it's clear that Tom's journey from Pontypridd to the top of the charts was just the beginning. The world may have known him for his hits like "It's Not Unusual" and "She's a Lady," but Tom was only getting started. His career was about to take him to places he never imagined—Las Vegas residencies, Grammy Awards, and, eventually, a knighthood.

But that's a story for another chapter. For now, let's raise a glass to the man who taught us that it's never too late to chase your dreams—and that, sometimes, all it takes is the right song and a little shake of the hips to change your life forever. Cheers to you, Sir Tom Jones!

3

The Golden Era – The Swinging Sixties

Ah, the Swinging Sixties—a time of miniskirts, Beatlemania, and enough hairspray to make your coif survive a hurricane. But while the world was grooving to rock 'n' roll and screaming for mop-topped boys from Liverpool, there was another voice making waves—a voice so powerful, so soulful, and so downright *irresistible* that it could shake the foundations of the charts. Yes, it was none other than Tom Jones, the man who stole hearts with his voice and shook things up with his, well, let's just say *unusual* hip movements.

Welcome to the Golden Era of Tom Jones, a time when our favorite Welsh crooner became an unstoppable force, turning every radio, club, and concert hall into his personal playground.

Tom Jones' Impact on the Music Scene in the 1960s

By the mid-1960s, the music scene was in full swing, with the British Invasion taking over America, and new sounds emerging faster than you could say "flower power." But amidst all the psychedelic rock and folk ballads, there was one man who stood out like a flash of neon amidst tie-dye shirts—Tom Jones, the Welsh dynamo with a voice that could melt butter (and hearts) with just one note.

Tom wasn't just another singer riding the wave of pop culture; he was a *force of nature*. While other artists were experimenting with jangly guitars and free love anthems, Tom came onto the scene with a sound that was as bold as his velvet suits and as powerful as his famous hip swivels. It wasn't long before his voice became the soundtrack to the decade.

His performances were electrifying—part gospel preacher, part rock star, and part heartthrob. Tom brought an intensity to the stage that left audiences breathless. He wasn't just singing; he was pouring every ounce of emotion into each song, turning every performance into an event you couldn't bear to miss.

And boy, did the fans notice. They flocked to see him live, swooning, screaming, and (legend has it) occasionally tossing their underwear on stage—a tradition that Tom, ever the gentleman, accepted with a cheeky grin and a wink. Because really, who could resist the allure of that deep baritone crooning, "It's Not Unusual"?

Iconic Hits: "Delilah," "What's New Pussycat?", and "Green, Green Grass of Home"

Tom Jones' secret sauce wasn't just his voice—it was also his knack for picking (and sometimes co-writing) songs that would stand the test of time. The 1960s were a whirlwind of hits for Tom, and it seemed like every time you turned on the radio, his voice was there, serenading you with yet another chart-topping single.

First up, let's talk about the dramatic and oh-so-theatrical "Delilah." This song became an anthem for heartbroken lovers everywhere, with its story of betrayal, passion, and, let's face it, a bit of murderous intent. (I mean, who knew a song about stabbing someone could be so catchy?) When Tom belted out the chorus—"*My, my, my, Delilah!*"—audiences couldn't help but sing along. It was raw, it was dramatic, and it was pure Tom Jones.

Then there was the quirky and playful "What's New Pussycat?". Now, if there was ever a song that could get stuck in your head for days, it's this one. The combination of Tom's flirtatious delivery and Burt Bacharach's bouncy melody was a match made in pop heaven. You could practically hear the wink in Tom's voice as he sang, making listeners swoon and smile all at once. It became an instant classic, even inspiring a movie of the same name, proving that Tom wasn't just a singer—he was a cultural phenomenon.

But let's not forget the tear-jerker of the bunch, "Green, Green

Grass of Home." This song showed a softer side of Tom, one that was nostalgic, tender, and deeply moving. Singing about a longing for home, Tom struck a chord with fans around the world, especially those who were far from their own hometowns. It became a global hit and remains one of his most beloved songs to this day. And honestly, who doesn't get a little misty-eyed when they hear that iconic opening line: "The old home town looks the same..." (Go on, I'll wait while you grab a tissue.)

Touring the World and Becoming a Household Name

With hit after hit lighting up the charts, it was time for Tom to take his show on the road—literally. The 1960s were a blur of airports, hotels, and sold-out arenas. Tom wasn't just content to conquer the UK charts; he was on a mission to bring his music to every corner of the globe. And boy, did he succeed.

Tom's world tours were nothing short of spectacular. He was the man of the hour, the one everyone wanted to see live. From London to Los Angeles, Tokyo to Toronto, fans lined up for hours just for a chance to see him in action. His shows were legendary—packed with energy, emotion, and enough charisma to power a small city.

One of the most memorable tours was when Tom took America by storm. He wasn't just playing clubs and theaters; he was filling iconic venues like Madison Square Garden and the Hollywood Bowl. The Americans couldn't get enough of him, and Tom quickly became a household name across the pond. His appearances on *The Ed Sullivan Show* and *The Tonight Show Starring Johnny Carson* turned him into a staple of American television, bringing his voice and charm into millions of living rooms.

Tom's Las Vegas shows, however, were the stuff of legend. He became a regular at Caesar's Palace, where he performed to packed houses night after night. The glitz, the glamour, the hip-shaking—Tom was in his element. The shows were equal parts concert and party, with Tom turning the Strip into his personal playground. It was during these years that Tom became known as the "King of Las Vegas," a title that would follow him for decades.

The Legacy of the Swinging Sixties

By the end of the 1960s, Tom Jones had done more than just leave his mark—he had *redefined* what it meant to be a pop star. He wasn't just about the music; he was a showman, an entertainer, a heartthrob who could make you laugh, cry, and dance all in the same show. His blend of pop, rock, and soul was a breath of fresh air in a decade that was bursting with musical innovation.

But more than anything, Tom Jones was *fun*. In a time when the world was dealing with social upheaval, political turmoil, and cultural revolutions, Tom was there to remind us that sometimes, all you need is a good song, a strong voice, and maybe a little hip shake to make everything feel alright.

The 1960s may have been the decade of The Beatles, The Rolling Stones, and Jimi Hendrix, but Tom Jones carved out a space all his own. He wasn't trying to be the coolest or the edgiest—he was simply being himself. And that's what made him so special.

Looking Ahead

As the 1970s approached, Tom was ready to take his career to the next level. The Swinging Sixties may have launched him into stardom, but the best was yet to come. With his voice as strong as ever and his fan base growing by the day, Tom was about to embark on the next chapter of his incredible journey.

But that, dear reader, is a story for another chapter. So, let's turn the page and get ready to see what happens when Tom takes on the world of Vegas showrooms, disco beats, and—believe it or not—knightings from the Queen herself.

The Las Vegas Years: Tom Jones at Caesar's Palace

By the time the 1970s rolled around, Tom Jones had already taken the music world by storm with hits like "It's Not Unusual" and "Delilah." But just when everyone thought they'd seen it all, Tom had a new trick up his well-tailored sleeve. He packed his bags, shook off the rainy skies of Britain, and set his sights on the bright, neon lights of Las Vegas. If there's one thing Tom knew how to do, it was putting on a show—*and oh boy, what a show it was.*

Caesar's Palace: The Start of a Legendary Residency

Las Vegas was already known as the place where legends went to either make or break their careers. But for Tom, it was nothing short of a rebirth—a *Sex Bomb* explosion of glamour, glitz, and, of course, those signature hip swivels. In 1967, Tom Jones kicked off his first residency at Caesar's Palace, one of the most iconic venues on the Strip. The minute Tom stepped onto that stage, the audience was hooked. It wasn't just a concert; it was a full-blown *experience.*

Back in the day, a Vegas residency was like a badge of honor for entertainers. It meant you were no longer just a pop star—you were a showman, an icon, a performer who could command the stage night after night. Tom took on this challenge with gusto, transforming himself from chart-topping heartthrob into the ultimate Vegas showman.

His shows were an intoxicating blend of his classic hits, soulful ballads, and high-energy dance numbers. Dressed in sharp, tailored suits (and later, some rather daring open-chested shirts that left little to the imagination), Tom brought the heat to

Caesar's Palace. It wasn't long before his performances became the hottest ticket in town. Celebrities, high rollers, and devoted fans alike flocked to see the Welshman with the voice that could shake the rafters.

The Signature Moves: Hip-Shaking and Heartbreaking

Let's talk about those hips, shall we? Because, let's be honest, they deserve their own chapter. Tom Jones' hip-shaking performances became the stuff of legend in Vegas. Imagine this: Tom, microphone in hand, belting out "She's a Lady" while his hips moved in ways that should probably come with a warning label. The audience? Utterly mesmerized. There was something about the way he moved that made the crowd go wild—especially the ladies.

In fact, Tom's hips were so famous that they became almost as iconic as his voice. Women would scream, faint, and, yes, throw their undergarments onto the stage in sheer adoration. Legend has it that the staff at Caesar's Palace once had to invest in extra-large laundry hampers just to keep up with the mountain of bras, panties, and even hotel room keys tossed at Tom during his performances. One night, a fan even flung a pair of diamond-encrusted panties onto the stage—talk about sparkling devotion!

But here's the thing: Tom never let it go to his head. He was always gracious, always appreciative, and always ready to flash that cheeky grin that said, "Oh, don't stop now." The underwear? He took it all in stride, even joking in interviews that he'd considered opening a lingerie shop with all the items he'd collected over the years.

Celebrity Encounters: When the Stars Align in Vegas

Las Vegas wasn't just about the fans—it was a playground for the stars, and Tom quickly found himself rubbing shoulders with the crème de la crème of Hollywood. If the walls of Caesar's Palace could talk, they'd probably spill secrets that would make the tabloids blush. But for Tom, these celebrity encounters were just another night at the office.

One of his most legendary friendships was with none other than Elvis Presley. The King of Rock 'n' Roll himself was a huge fan of Tom's, and the admiration was mutual. Elvis would often sneak into Tom's shows, disguised in sunglasses and a hat, to watch his friend perform. The two would hang out backstage after the show, swapping stories, sharing a few laughs, and even jamming together into the wee hours of the morning. Tom later admitted that some of his fondest memories were of those late-night sessions with Elvis. "We'd sing anything that came to mind," Tom once recalled. 'Elvis was the only person who could out-sing me at 4 a.m. after a few drinks."

But Elvis wasn't the only star drawn to Tom's magnetic performances. Frank Sinatra, Sammy Davis Jr., and Dean Martin were all known to stop by for a taste of the Tom Jones magic. There was something about Tom's show that had everyone from A-list actors to mob bosses (hey, it was Vegas in the '70s!) wanting a front-row seat.

Wild Stories from the Vegas Years: When Tom Ruled the Strip

Ah, the Vegas years—where the line between reality and myth often blurred. There are enough wild stories from Tom's time on the Strip to fill a book (or three), but here are a few of the juiciest.

One night, after a particularly electric performance of "Thunderball," a fan was so overwhelmed that she literally climbed onto the stage, wrapped her arms around Tom, and refused to let go. Security rushed in, but Tom, ever the charmer, simply winked and said, "Let the lady stay, it's not unusual to have a bit of fun." The crowd erupted in laughter, and the fan was gently escorted back to her seat—though not before getting a kiss on the cheek from Tom.

Another night, Frank Sinatra himself dared Tom to perform an entire set while holding a martini. Never one to back down from a challenge, Tom did just that—singing his heart out with a glass in hand, only stopping occasionally to take a sip. The audience loved it, and Sinatra, who was watching from the wings, declared, "Now *that's* how you do Vegas."

But it wasn't all glitz and glamour. Tom was known for his dedication to his craft. He would spend hours rehearsing, making sure every note, every hip swivel, and every wink was perfectly timed. His goal was simple: to give the audience a night they'd never forget. And boy, did he deliver.

Reinventing Himself in the City of Lights

Tom's Vegas years weren't just about sequins, showgirls, and champagne. They were also a time of reinvention. While some artists came to Vegas to retire Tom came to thrive. The city gave him the creative freedom to experiment with his music, try new arrangements, and reinvent old classics. It was here that he developed the stage presence that would define the rest of his career.

As the 1980s approached, the music world was changing, but Tom was ready for whatever came next. He left Vegas with more than just a collection of fans and fond memories—he left with a new understanding of who he was as an artist. He was no longer just a singer; he was an entertainer in the truest sense of the word. And as he moved on to conquer the next chapters of his career, he carried the lessons of Vegas with him: *be bold, be fearless, and never forget to have a little fun along the way.*

The Legacy of the Las Vegas Years

Tom's time in Las Vegas was more than just a few years of glitzy shows—it was a defining era that turned him into a global icon. Even today, when people think of the golden age of Vegas, they think of Tom Jones, shaking his hips and belting out hits with that unmistakable voice.

So here's to the Vegas years: the wild nights, the celebrity encounters, and the endless encores. Because, as Tom Jones showed us, when life gives you a stage, you better put on one hell of a show.

Now, let's move on to the next chapter, where Tom takes his talents beyond the Strip and into the hearts of fans around the world. Because for Tom Jones, the show never really ends—it just gets better.

4

Musical Evolution & Reinvention

Surviving the Changing Tides: Tom's Transformation Over the Decades

Let's face it: the music industry can be a fickle beast. One minute you're on top of the charts, and the next, you're yesterday's news. But if there's one thing that Tom Jones knows how to do—besides making hearts flutter with that deep baritone—it's how to stay relevant. From the funky disco era of the 1970s to the rock-fueled '80s and the neon-splattered, synth-heavy '90s, Tom has weathered every musical storm like the true "Thunderball" he is.

When most artists from his era were beginning to fade into obscurity, Tom was just getting started. In the world of music, it's "Not Unusual" (sorry, had to!) for careers to burn bright and fizzle fast. But Tom was determined to not just survive, but thrive—and he did so with a mix of reinvention, experimentation, and a whole lot of hip swiveling.

The 1970s: Disco Fever & Las Vegas Swagger

Ah, the '70s: a time of disco balls, bell-bottoms, and some questionable fashion choices. But for Tom Jones, it was also a period of reinvention. After conquering the charts in the '60s with hits like "Delilah" and "What's New Pussycat?", Tom needed to find a way to keep that momentum going. So, what did he do? He packed his bags and set his sights on the glitziest place on Earth—Las Vegas.

By the early '70s, Tom had become the king of the Las Vegas strip. His residency at Caesar's Palace was legendary, with fans flocking to see him shake his hips and belt out his hits in that iconic voice. It was here that Tom truly embraced his inner showman. He wasn't just singing; he was performing. His shows were a whirlwind of sequined outfits, flashy lights, and, of course, those infamous underwear-throwing fans. (Seriously, it's not every day you see women tossing their knickers at a performer, but for Tom, it was just another Tuesday night!)

While the glitzy Vegas scene was a great gig, Tom knew he couldn't rest on his laurels. The disco wave was sweeping the music world, and Tom, ever the chameleon, decided to dip his toes into the funky waters. Songs like "Do You Take This Man" and "Darlin'" brought a touch of disco flair to his repertoire, proving that Tom could groove with the best of them. While he never went full "Disco Inferno," he found a way to blend his soulful roots with the shimmering sounds of the era.

The 1980s: Rock 'n' Roll Reinvention

As the '70s came to a close, disco began to die down, and rock 'n' roll took center stage. But did Tom hang up his microphone and retreat to the comfort of his Vegas residency? Absolutely not! This was Tom Jones, after all—the man who could sing the phone book and still make it sound like a hit.

In the 1980s, Tom leaned into a rock-inspired sound, embracing the grittier, edgier vibe of the decade. He traded in the sequins for leather jackets and let his hair grow a little wilder. (Okay, maybe not quite as wild as some of those hair metal bands, but you get the idea.) His deep, soulful voice adapted beautifully to the rock scene, proving that, like a fine wine, it only got better with age.

One of his most memorable tracks from this era was "Kiss," a cover of Prince's iconic hit. Now, some might say it was a bold move to cover Prince, but Tom didn't just cover it—he *owned* it. With a sultry swagger and that unmistakable growl, Tom's version of "Kiss" became a hit in its own right, introducing him to a whole new generation of fans who were probably still in diapers when "It's Not Unusual" came out.

But Tom's foray into rock wasn't just about covers. He embraced the decade's sound, collaborating with artists and producers who helped him stay on the cutting edge of the music scene. He even managed to make a splash on MTV, a channel typically dominated by the likes of Madonna and Michael Jackson. Tom's music videos, featuring his signature dance moves and undeniable charisma, were a breath of fresh air among the flashy neon and over-the-top visuals of the time.

The 1990s: Reloading for a New Generation

By the time the '90s rolled around, many of Tom's contemporaries had faded into obscurity, but not our man Tom. Oh no, he was just getting started. If the '90s had a theme song for Tom, it would've been "I'm Still Standing" (though that's Elton's song, but you get the point). Tom was determined to prove that he wasn't just an oldies act—he was a musical force to be reckoned with.

The turning point came in 1999 with the release of *Reload*, an album that paired Tom with contemporary artists for a series of duets. On paper, it might have seemed like a desperate attempt to stay relevant, but in reality, it was a masterstroke of reinvention. Tom collaborated with everyone from The Cardigans to Robbie Williams, infusing his timeless voice with modern sounds and styles.

One standout track from *Reload* was "Burning Down the House" with The Cardigans. The song was a quirky, high-energy cover that breathed new life into the Talking Heads classic. It was a perfect match: Tom's deep, powerful voice against The Cardigans' indie pop vibe created a sound that was fresh, fun, and undeniably catchy.

Then there was "Mama Told Me Not to Come," a rollicking duet with Welsh rockers Stereophonics. The song became an instant hit, climbing the UK charts and proving that Tom still had what it took to top the charts—even after four decades in the business. The secret to his success? Tom's willingness to adapt, to experiment, and to collaborate with younger artists who brought a new energy to his music.

The Timeless Appeal of Tom's Voice and Charisma

So, what is it about Tom Jones that has kept him in the limelight for so long? In a world where musical trends come and go faster than you can say "Sex Bomb," how has Tom managed to stay relevant through it all? The answer lies in that voice—rich, soulful, and as smooth as a glass of aged whisky. Whether he's singing a tender ballad, rocking out with a power anthem, or getting funky with a dance track, Tom's voice is the constant that ties it all together.

But it's not just about the voice. Tom's charisma is the stuff of legend. He's the kind of performer who could sing the ingredients on a cereal box and still have the audience eating out of the palm of his hand. Whether he's crooning to a room full of swooning fans or belting out a power anthem, he does it all with a twinkle in his eye and a smile that says, "I'm having just as much fun as you are."

Tom Jones has proven that while musical tastes may change, there will always be a place for real talent. His ability to adapt, to experiment, and to stay true to himself has kept him in the spotlight for more than six decades. And let's be honest—who wouldn't want to still be rocking out on stage, shaking their hips, and making fans scream at 80 years old?

As Tom once sang, "You Can Leave Your Hat On," because this legend isn't going anywhere. And with a career like his, who would ever want him to?

The Comeback King: The Rise of Sir Tom Jones

If there's one thing we've learned about Tom Jones over the years, it's that you can never count him out. Just when you think you've seen it all, he comes back stronger, bolder, and cooler than ever. And nowhere is that more apparent than in the 2000s, a decade that proved to the world that Tom Jones isn't just an icon of the past—he's a musical force to be reckoned with. Whether collaborating with artists half his age, exploring new genres, or embracing his roots, Tom's comeback story is a lesson in how to age like fine wine—just with a lot more swagger.

Reload: The Comeback Starts Here

By the late '90s, Tom Jones was already a living legend, but the world of music was changing fast. Enter the 2000s: boy bands, pop divas, and the rise of hip-hop were taking over the airwaves. But Tom, ever the master of reinvention, knew it wasn't quite time to hang up his microphone just yet. Instead, he decided to take a different approach. Why not collaborate with the new kids on the block?

Cue *Reload* (1999), an album that was aptly named because it truly reloaded Tom's career, launching him into the 21st century with a bang. The idea was simple but brilliant: take that unmistakable Tom Jones voice and mix it with contemporary artists across various genres. The result? Magic.

The album featured collaborations with the likes of The Cardigans on "Burning Down the House" (yes, that Talking Heads classic), Stereophonics on "Mama Told Me Not to Come," and even a cheeky duet with Robbie Williams on "Are You Gonna Go My Way?" But the crown jewel of the album was the smash hit "Sex Bomb," a funky, sultry track co-created with Wyclef Jean that quickly became a dancefloor staple. If anyone doubted that Tom still had it, this was their answer: he wasn't just back—he was a *Sex Bomb*, baby!

Reload was a massive hit, reaching number one on the UK charts and going multi-platinum. It introduced Tom to a whole new generation of fans who weren't even born when he was crooning "It's Not Unusual" in the '60s. Suddenly, Tom Jones was cool again. And just like that, the Comeback King was born.

24 Hours: A Fresh Sound for a New Decade

With the success of *Reload* under his belt, Tom could have easily sat back and coasted on his newfound popularity. But that's not Tom's style. No, he wanted to push himself even further. And so, in 2008, he released *24 Hours*, an album that saw him moving away from the collaborations of *Reload* and focusing on original material that showcased a more mature, reflective side.

But let's be clear: this wasn't an album for easy-listening Sunday afternoons. 24 Hours had the energy and edge of a man who, even in his late sixties, was still full of fire. Tracks like "If He Should Ever Leave You" and "Give a Little Love" combined that classic Tom Jones power with modern production, proving that he could still hold his own against the pop stars of the day.

Critics praised 24 Hours for its boldness and authenticity. It was an album that reflected where Tom was at this point in his life—more introspective but still filled with that signature Tom Jones passion. It was like he was saying, "I may have a few more wrinkles, but I can still bring the house down." And you know what? He did.

Praise & Blame: Going Back to His Roots

If Reload was about proving he could keep up with the young guns and 24 Hours was a showcase of his contemporary relevance, then Praise & Blame (2010) was something entirely different. This time, Tom stripped everything back—no flashy duets, no funky dance beats. Just raw, honest music that went straight to the soul.

For Praise & Blame, Tom took a deep dive into the world of blues, gospel, and Americana, drawing on the music that had inspired him as a young boy in Wales. The album was recorded live in the studio, giving it a gritty, authentic feel. Tracks like "What Good Am I?" and "Did Trouble Me" showcased a side of Tom we hadn't seen in years—vulnerable, reflective, and, dare we say it, a bit *preachy* (but in the best possible way).

Critics were floored. *Praise & Blame* was hailed as one of the best albums of Tom's career. It was proof that, even after five decades in the business, Tom could still surprise us. And perhaps most importantly, it showed that he was still willing to take risks, even when he had nothing left to prove.

A Knighthood for the King

As if chart-topping albums and sold-out concerts weren't enough, the ultimate honor came in 2006 when Tom was knighted by Queen Elizabeth II for his services to music. That's right, folks: he went from being the boy from Pontypridd to *Sir* Tom Jones. It's not unusual (sorry, we had to) to see artists get recognized for their contributions, but for Tom, this was something truly special.

The knighthood was a culmination of everything Tom had achieved over the years. It wasn't just about the hits, the awards, or the legions of adoring fans—it was about a career that had spanned over four decades, full of reinvention, resilience, and, above all, staying true to himself. With that shiny new "Sir" title, Tom was officially music royalty.

But don't think for a second that being knighted made Tom slow down. If anything, it only fueled his passion to keep going. He continued touring, performing for packed arenas, and recording new music, proving that age is just a number when you've got the heart of a lion (or in Tom's case, a Welsh dragon).

The Legend Continues

By the end of the 2000s, Tom Jones had not only reclaimed his throne as one of the greatest voices in music but had also established himself as an artist who could evolve with the times. He wasn't just a relic of the '60s or a nostalgia act for those who remembered his Vegas days. He was a true chameleon, adapting to new musical landscapes while still maintaining that signature sound.

Whether he was belting out bluesy gospel tunes on *Praise & Blame* or grooving to a dance beat with Wyclef Jean, Tom showed us that it's never too late to reinvent yourself. He was living proof that you could still be a "Sex Bomb" well into your seventies and that life truly begins at... well, whenever you decide it does.

So, what's the secret to Tom Jones' seemingly endless energy? Maybe it's that he's always had a bit of a rebellious streak, refusing to let the industry pigeonhole him. Maybe it's the sheer joy he gets from performing, the electric connection he has with his fans. Or maybe it's just that unmistakable voice that still has the power to make us swoon.

Whatever the secret, one thing's for sure: Tom Jones is, and always will be, the Comeback King. So, let's raise a glass (or maybe a pair of knickers) to the man who's proven time and again that it's never too late to *Reload*, live life like it's 24 *Hours*, and always find time to give a little *Praise & Blame*. Cheers to you, Sir Tom—may you keep on swinging for years to come!

5

Tom Jones, the Entertainer

By now, we all know that Tom Jones has a voice that can melt hearts, light up a room, and probably shatter a few wine glasses along the way. But there's more to Sir Tom than just that golden voice and those iconic hip swivels. If you think Tom Jones is just about "It's Not Unusual" and "Delilah," well, buckle up, because there's a whole other side to this Welsh wonder. Beyond the music, Tom has proven time and again that he's a true entertainer in every sense of the word.

From coaching young hopefuls on *The Voice UK* to making cameo appearances on TV shows, and even dabbling in a bit of Hollywood glamour, Tom's talents go far beyond the recording studio. And let's not forget his generous heart—because when it comes to giving back, Tom doesn't just sing the blues; he fights them too.

So, let's dive into the world of Tom Jones, the entertainer, where there's always something new behind the curtain.

Tom Jones, the TV Star: From Talk Shows to Talent Shows

Tom Jones on your television screen is like finding an unexpected £20 note in your pocket: always a delightful surprise. For decades, Tom has been a fixture on TV, proving that his charisma isn't just confined to the stage.

In the early days, he was a regular on popular shows like *Top of the Pops* and *The Ed Sullivan Show*, where he captivated audiences with his booming voice and cheeky smile. But Tom wasn't just content with singing his hits—he also knew how to work a crowd. Whether he was crooning "What's New Pussycat?" or joking with the show's hosts. Tom brought that special flair that left everyone wanting more.

However, his real TV breakthrough came in the late 1960s with his own variety show, *This Is Tom Jones.* For three seasons, audiences tuned in to watch Tom belt out songs, banter with celebrity guests, and perform skits that showcased his comedic timing. Yes, that's right—Tom Jones can be funny too! Who knew, right? *This Is Tom Jones* wasn't just a hit in the UK; it also became a sensation in the United States, turning Tom into an even bigger international star. The show even earned him a Golden Globe nomination, proving that Tom wasn't just a one-trick pony.

But if you thought Tom's TV career ended with his variety show, think again. Fast forward to 2012, and Sir Tom became one of the original coaches on *The Voice UK*. Now, if you've ever watched the show, you know it s full of dramatic chair turns, epic battles, and enough emotional backstories to rival any soap opera. And there, sitting in one of those spinning red chairs, was Tom Jones, the voice of experience, charm, and wisdom.

With his warm Welsh accent and that ever-present twinkle in his eye, Tom quickly became the heart and soul of *The Voice UK*. Week after week, he dished out advice, shared anecdotes from his storied career, and even broke into impromptu performances that had contestants (and sometimes his fellow coaches) starstruck. Let's face it: if Tom Jones tells you that you've got talent, you're basically set for life.

Tom Jones, the Actor: From Cameos to Cult Classics

Now, you might not immediately think of Tom Jones as an actor, but like any good entertainer, he's always up for a bit of fun in front of the camera. Over the years, Tom has made memorable cameos in movies and TV shows, proving that he's got more than just one trick up his velvet sleeves.

One of his most iconic film appearances was in Tim Burton's cult classic *Mars Attacks!* (1996). Yes, you read that right—Tom Jones fought off aliens! In the film, Tom plays himself, but with a twist: he's thrust into the middle of an alien invasion in Las Vegas. At one point, he saves the day with a group of survivors, all while singing "It's Not Unusual" with a flock of birds landing on his outstretched arms. If that doesn't scream "legend," what does?

Tom has also popped up in TV shows like *The Simpsons* and *Fresh*

Prince of Bel-Air, where he played a hilarious version of himself. Who could forget that scene with Carlton Banks dancing to "It's Not Unusual"? It's become an iconic moment in pop culture, cementing Tom's status as not just a singer but a true entertainer who knows how to have a laugh.

Tom Jones, the Philanthropist: Using His Voice for Good

While it's easy to get caught up in the glitz and glamour of Tom's career, there's another side to him that often goes unnoticed: his heart of gold. Tom has always believed in giving back, and over the years, he's lent his voice (literally and figuratively) to countless charitable causes.

One of Tom's most significant contributions has been his support of children's charities. As someone who grew up in a working-class family, Tom has never forgotten his roots. He's been involved with organizations like *Children in Need*, raising money and awareness for children facing tough challenges. Whether he's performing at benefit concerts or quietly making donations behind the scenes, Tom's generosity is as powerful as his voice.

And it's not just children's charities that have benefited from Tom's big heart. He's also been a staunch supporter of cancer research, hospice care, and relief efforts for those affected by natural disasters. When he performs at charity events, it's not just another gig for him; it's a chance to make a real difference. And let's be honest—when Tom Jones sings for a cause, wallets open, and hearts melt.

The Legacy of an Entertainer

So, what makes Tom Jones such an enduring figure in the entertainment world? Is it the voice? The charm? The ability to reinvent himself over and over? It's all of the above, plus something that can't quite be put into words. There's a reason why, after six decades in the spotlight, Tom is still here, still turning chairs on *The Voice UK*, still making us laugh on our favorite TV shows, and still making a difference with his charitable work.

Tom Jones isn't just an entertainer; he's an experience. Whether he's belting out "She's a Lady" to a crowd of thousands or cracking jokes with contestants on a talent show, Tom brings a unique blend of talent, warmth, and sincerity to everything he does. It's not just about being the best—it's about making people feel good, whether they're in a concert hall, watching at home, or receiving help from one of his charitable initiatives.

And let's not forget that Tom's story isn't over yet. Even as he moves into his 80s, there's still a sparkle in his eye and a song in his heart. He continues to inspire new generations of fans and artists alike, proving that age is just a number when you've got talent, passion, and a little bit of Welsh magic.

So, here's to Tom Jones—the man, the legend, the entertainer who's been making us laugh, dance, and sometimes cry since the 1960s. As long as he's around, it's safe to say that we'll never get tired of asking, "What's New, Pussycat?"

After all, in the world of entertainment, there's only one Tom Jones. And we wouldn't have it any other way.

Personal Life & Legacy - The Heart Behind the Voice

Behind the bright lights, glittering stages, and the sea of swooning fans lies the true heart of Tom Jones—a man who, despite his larger-than-life persona, has always cherished the simple things: love, family, and friendship. And let's be honest, no story about Tom would be complete without talking about the remarkable woman who stood by his side through thick and thin—Linda Trenchard, the love of his life.

The Love Story of Tom and Linda: "I'll Never Fall in Love Again" (Unless It's You)

Tom and Linda's love story is one that could inspire its own greatest hits album. The two were high school sweethearts who met in Pontypridd, Wales, when they were just 12 years old. Tom always said it was love at first sight, describing Linda as the most beautiful girl he had ever seen. She was his first love, his best friend, and his anchor. And, in true Tom Jones fashion, he swept her off her feet—probably with one of those signature hip swivels!

45

Their romance wasn't without its fair share of challenges. Tom and Linda married young—at just 16 years old—after discovering that they were expecting a child. At that time, Tom was far from being an international superstar. He was a young man working various odd jobs to make ends meet while trying to break into the music scene. But through it all, Linda remained his biggest supporter. While Tom was busy singing his heart out in smoky clubs, Linda was the one keeping the home fires burning.

The birth of their son, Mark, brought even more joy to their lives. Though times were tough, the couple shared an unbreakable bond. "It's Not Unusual" to hear stories of young love, but Tom and Linda's connection went beyond the ordinary. They weathered the ups and downs of life, showing that true love is about more than just passion—it's about partnership, patience, and trust.

The Price of Fame: "Delilah" and the Other Women

Let's face it—being married to one of the most desirable men on the planet couldn't have been easy. Tom's rise to fame in the 1960s and '70s brought its fair share of temptations. With legions of adoring fans throwing themselves (and sometimes their underwear) at him, Tom's life on the road was nothing short of a whirlwind.

Tom has been open about his infidelities during those years, admitting that he was unfaithful to Linda on numerous occasions. It was something that weighed on him, but he always maintained that Linda was his one true love. "She's a Lady" wasn't just a song; it was his way of acknowledging the strength, grace, and resilience of the woman who stood by him through it all. Linda chose to stay with Tom despite his indiscretions, a testament to the deep bond they shared.

In interviews, Tom described Linda as his rock—the one person who truly understood him. Despite the media frenzy, the touring, and the crazy rock 'n' roll lifestyle, Tom would always come back home to Linda. She was his constant, his North Star, and the one person who kept him grounded.

Family Matters: "The Green, Green Grass of Home"

For all the glamour and glitter of Tom's career, home was always where his heart truly lay. When he wasn't busy performing on stages around the world, Tom cherished the simple moments of family life. His son, Mark, would later become his manager, a partnership that brought the father-son duo even closer.

Tom's love for his family extended beyond his immediate circle. Friends and fellow musicians often spoke of his generosity and loyalty. Whether it was sharing a laugh backstage or offering a helping hand to those in need, Tom has always been the kind of person who values genuine connections. The warmth you hear in his voice? It's not just for show—it's a reflection of who he truly is.

Tom's ability to stay connected to his roots is one of the reasons fans adore him. Despite achieving international fame, he never forgot where he came from. He often returned to Wales, not just to perform, but to reconnect with the people and places that shaped him. After all, you can take the boy out of Pontypridd, but you can't take Pontypridd out of the boy.

The Love of His Life: Saying Goodbye to Linda

In 2016, Tom faced one of the toughest moments of his life when Linda passed away after a short battle with cancer. They had been married for nearly 60 years. Losing Linda was devastating for Tom. He described her as the love of his life, his best friend, and his greatest source of strength. In interviews following her death, he spoke candidly about the profound grief he felt.

The man who had sung so many songs about love, passion, and heartbreak was now living through his own. It's hard to imagine Tom without his beloved Linda, but he found a way to carry on, just as she would have wanted him to. In her memory, Tom continued to perform, pouring all of his emotion into his music. For him, singing wasn't just a career—it was a way to heal, to remember, and to honor the love they shared.

Reflections on a Legendary Career: "Still the One"

Tom Jones' legacy is not just about the music, the awards, or the sold-out shows. It's about a man who, despite the fame and fortune, remained true to himself. Even as he entered his later years, Tom refused to slow down. In his 70s, he released albums like *Praise & Blame* and *Spirit in the Room*, exploring deeper, more soulful sounds. His voice, still rich and powerful, proved that he was far from a relic of the past. He was, and still is, a force to be reckoned with.

Tom has inspired countless artists, from Elvis Presley (who was a huge fan) to modern stars like Ed Sheeran and Adele. But more importantly, he's inspired his fans to embrace life with passion, resilience, and a little bit of cheekiness. After all, who else could get away with singing "You Can Leave Your Hat On" with such gusto?

Tom's Enduring Legacy: "If I Only Knew"

What makes Tom Jones truly remarkable isn't just his voice or his charisma—it's his enduring spirit. He's a man who's lived a life full of highs and lows, successes and stumbles, yet always managed to come out on top. His ability to reinvent himself, whether it was swinging with the mods in the '60s or collaborating with modern artists in the 2000s, is a testament to his versatility.

But perhaps Tom's greatest legacy isn't found in the awards he's won or the records he's sold. It's in the hearts of the millions who've been touched by his music. Whether you've danced to "Sex Bomb" at a wedding, cried to "Green, Green Grass of Home," or belted out "Delilah" at karaoke, Tom's songs have become a soundtrack to our lives.

The Final Bow: "I'm Coming Home"

As Tom continues to perform well into his 80s, he shows no signs of stopping. He's the epitome of grace, grit, and timeless talent. Whether he's singing in front of thousands or simply enjoying a quiet moment at home, Tom remains true to himself.

And maybe that's the secret to his enduring appeal. For Tom, it's never been just about the fame or the money. It's about the music, the love, and the connections he's made along the way. So, the next time you hear one of his songs on the radio, remember that behind that iconic voice is a man who has lived, loved, and left an indelible mark on the world.

Here's to you, Sir Tom Jones—a legend, a lover, and a legacy that will live on forever.

6

Fun Facts & Trivia – Behind the Legend

om Jones is not just a music icon—he's a living
legend with a treasure trove of stories that span
over six decades in show business. From unexpected
encounters with other superstars to quirky backstage moments
and wild fan interactions there's more to Sir Tom than just his
hits. Let's pull back the curtain and dive into some of the lesser-
known (and totally entertaining) stories that make Tom Jones
the *legend* he is today.

Little-Known Facts About Tom Jones

1. **The Man with the Golden Voice Was Almost... A Brick-
   layer?** Before he became the iconic singer we know today,
   Tom was almost headed for a career in construction. As a
   teenager, he worked as a builder's laborer to make ends
   meet, but he was never quite cut out for the 9-to-5 grind.
   Lucky for us, he decided to pursue music instead. Can you

imagine Tom Jones in a hard hat, belting out "It's Not Unusual" while laying bricks? Neither can we!

2. **He Once Sang the James Bond Theme in His Underwear** Recording the iconic theme for the James Bond film *Thunderball* was a huge moment in Tom's career. But here's the twist: he was so committed to hitting that final high note that he nearly passed out in the recording booth. Rumor has it, he was belting out the song with such intensity that he ripped off his clothes to finish the take. Now that's what we call dedication! (Though we don't recommend trying that at home.)

3. **The Hip Shake That Almost Got Him Arrested** Tom's signature hip-swinging dance moves were all the rage back in the '60s. However, not everyone was a fan of his pelvis-thrusting performances. During a concert in New York, police actually warned him to tone down his moves or risk getting arrested for public indecency. Naturally, Tom did what any rock star would do—he swung those hips even harder!

4. **He Was Once Mistaken for Elvis Presley** At the height of his fame, Tom's deep baritone voice and slicked-back hair earned him comparisons to the King of Rock 'n' Roll. During a tour stop in Las Vegas, fans once mobbed Tom thinking he was Elvis! The two became good friends and often hung out in Sin City, swapping stories and, yes, even trading vocal tips. In fact, Elvis was known to cover Tom's songs during his own concerts.

5. **Tom's Famous Chest Hair Had Its Own Fan Club** Let's face it, Tom Jones is as famous for his deep voice as he is for his trademark chest hair. In the '70s, his open-chested shirts became a fashion statement, sparking a fan club devoted

entirely to his chest hair. Members would send fan mail with grooming tips, requests for shirt buttons to stay open, and even offers of homemade hair products. Talk about a *hair-raising* level of fandom!

Behind-the-Scenes Anecdotes

6. "It's Not Unusual" Almost Never Happened It's hard to imagine a world without "It's Not Unusual," but the song nearly never saw the light of day. It was initially written for Sandie Shaw, a popular singer at the time. When she turned it down, Tom recorded a demo, and the rest is history. The song's success catapulted Tom to instant stardom, proving that sometimes, one man's rejection is another man's golden opportunity.

7. The Secret to His Las Vegas Residency: A Stiff Drink Tom's legendary Las Vegas shows were known for their high energy and wild atmosphere. So, what was the secret behind his stamina during those late-night performances? Tom's pre-show ritual included sipping on a shot of whiskey to warm up his voice and calm his nerves. After all, when you're belting out "Delilah" to a packed crowd, a little liquid courage can go a long way!

8. The Time He Had to Dodge Flying Panties (and a Bra or Two) By now, everyone knows that Tom Jones concerts often turn into lingerie flinging fests. But did you know that Tom once got hit in the face by an airborne bra while performing "She's a Lady"? He famously quipped, "At least it wasn't a pair of trousers!" Fans throwing undergarments became such a phenomenon that Tom once joked about hiring a personal "panty catcher" on tour.

9. Tom's Surprising Friendship with Janis Joplin Tom and rock legend Janis Joplin may seem like an odd pairing, but the two became fast friends after performing a duet on Tom's TV show *This Is Tom Jones*. Backstage, they bonded over a shared love of music and a few stiff drinks. Janis reportedly told Tom, "You've got more soul than a white boy should have!" High praise from the Queen of Psychedelic Rock!

10. He Lost His Iconic Voice... for a Day During a particularly grueling tour, Tom's voice suddenly gave out just before a big concert. Panicking, his team tried everything from hot tea to honey and even an old Welsh remedy involving leeks (don't ask). Just before showtime, Tom miraculously regained his voice. He powered through the set and even managed to hit the high notes in "I (Who Have Nothing)." Talk about a *miracle of music*!

Memorable Moments on Stage

11. Performing for Royalty (and Making Them Blush) Tom has had the honor of performing for British royalty multiple times. During one event, he performed "Sex Bomb" for an audience that included the Queen herself. Let's just say, the look on Her Majesty's face was priceless! Tom later admitted that he was more nervous about performing that cheeky number than any other song in his repertoire.

12. The Time He Danced with a Giant Puppet on Stage In the 1990s, Tom took his showmanship to the next level by incorporating some wild stage props. During one memorable concert, he performed "You Can Leave Your Hat On" alongside a giant, life-sized puppet. The audience loved it, but Tom confessed that dancing with a puppet was harder than performing with a live band!

13. His Most Emotional Performance: A Tribute to Linda One of the most moving moments in Tom's career came after the passing of his beloved wife, Linda. During a concert in London, Tom dedicated "I'll Never Fall in Love Again" to her memory. The performance brought both him and the audience to tears. Tom later said it was one of the hardest yet most meaningful performances of his life.

14. When Tom Was Asked to Perform... at a Biker Rally Tom's appeal transcends genres, but even he was surprised when he was invited to perform at a massive biker rally in the 1980s. Surrounded by leather-clad fans and roaring motorcycles, Tom delivered a powerhouse performance that ended with the bikers chanting "Tom! Tom! Tom!" Who knew that "Delilah" could bring a crowd of bikers to their feet?

The Man, The Myth, The Legend

Tom Jones has been rocking the stage, melting hearts, and making headlines for over six decades. Whether he's belting out "Kiss" with Prince-like swagger or serenading fans with the soulful "Green, Green Grass of Home," Tom remains one of the most beloved figures in music. And while we may never run out of fascinating stories about this Welsh wonder, one thing's for sure: Sir Tom Jones will always leave us wanting more.

So next time you find yourself humming "It's Not Unusual" or dancing to "Sex Bomb," remember that behind those iconic hits are countless stories of laughter, love, and a whole lot of fun. Here's to you, Tom—thank you for the music, the memories, and the unforgettable moments.

7

Trivia Quiz – Are You a True Tom Fan?

Welcome to the ultimate Tom Jones fan quiz! Think you know everything about the Welsh legend who stole our hearts with that unforgettable voice, those hip-shaking moves, and timeless hits? Put your knowledge to the test with this fun, 20-question quiz that dives deep into Tom's life, career, and musical journey.

Grab a pen (or just your brain power) and see how many you can get right. Remember, no cheating! Answers and explanations are at the end. Let's find out if you're a "Sex Bomb" level fan or if you need to spend some more time listening to "It's Not Unusual" on repeat.

The Tom Jones Trivia Quiz

1. What was Tom Jones' first hit single that shot him to fame in 1965?
   a) "Delilah"
   b) "It's Not Unusual"
   c) "What's New Pussycat?"
   d) "Green, Green Grass of Home"

2. In which year was Tom Jones knighted by Queen Elizabeth II for his services to music?
   a) 2000
   b) 2006
   c) 2010
   d) 2012

3. Tom Jones' real name is...
   a) Thomas John Woodward
   b) Thomas James Jones
   c) Jonathan Tom Harris
   d) William Thomas Edwards

4. Which James Bond film featured Tom singing the theme song?
   a) *Goldfinger*
   b) *Thunderball*
   c) *You Only Live Twice*
   d) *Live and Let Die*

5. What was the name of Tom's 1999 comeback album that featured duets with artists like The Cardigans and Robbie

Williams?
   a) *Reload*
   b) *Revival*
   c) *Rewind*
   d) *Return*

6. Tom was a coach on which popular talent show in the UK?
   a) *The X Factor*
   b) *Britain's Got Talent*
   c) *The Voice UK*
   d) *Pop Idol*

7. In which country was Tom Jones born?
   a) Scotland
   b) Wales
   c) England
   d) Ireland

8. Who did Tom Jones collaborate with for the hit song "Sex Bomb"?
   a) Prince
   b) Wyclef Jean
   c) Art of Noise
   d) Mousse T

9. Which song did Tom famously perform while dancing with a puppet on his TV show?
   a) "You Can Leave Your Hat On"
   b) "Delilah"
   c) "She's a Lady"
   d) "What's New Pussycat?"

10. Tom dedicated which emotional song to his late wife, Linda, during a concert after her passing?

   a) "Without Love"

   b) "I'll Never Fall in Love Again"

   c) "Green, Green Grass of Home"

   d) "Till"

11. How old was Tom when he first became a father?

   a) 16

   b) 18

   c) 20

   d) 22

12. Tom recorded the song "Burning Down the House" with which band?

   a) Coldplay

   b) The Cardigans

   c) Stereophonics

   d) Talking Heads

13. What was the name of Tom's beloved wife, who he was married to for nearly 60 years?

   a) Mary

   b) Linda

   c) Susan

   d) Elizabeth

14. In what year did Tom Jones release his iconic hit "Delilah"?

   a) 1965

   b) 1967

   c) 1968

d) 1970

15. Tom's song "Green, Green Grass of Home" became an international hit, but it was originally a...

a) Country song

b) Gospel song

c) Rock 'n' roll song

d) Jazz standard

16. Which famous American singer was one of Tom's close friends and even performed covers of Tom's songs?

a) Frank Sinatra

b) Elvis Presley

c) Ray Charles

d) Johnny Cash

17. Tom's Las Vegas residency made him a household name in the entertainment capital. In which decade did he start performing there?

a) 1960s

b) 1970s

c) 1980s

d) 1990s

18. Tom once appeared on which classic animated TV show, singing a duet with a cartoon character?

a) *The Simpsons*

b) *Scooby-Doo*

c) *Family Guy*

d) *South Park*

19. Which song did Tom Jones famously perform at the Queen's Diamond Jubilee in 2012?

a) "It's Not Unusual"

b) "Delilah"

c) "Kiss"

d) "She's a Lady"

20. Which hit song features the lyrics: "Spy on me baby, use satellite..."?

a) "Delilah"

b) "Sex Bomb"

c) "I'll Never Fall in Love Again"

d) "What's New Pussycat?"

Answers and Explanations

1. **b) "It's Not Unusual"** – The song that launched Tom's career and made him an international star.

2. **b) 2006** – Sir Tom was knighted in 2006 for his contribution to music.

3. **a) Thomas John Woodward** – That's Tom's birth name before he adopted his famous stage name.

4. **b)** *Thunderball* – Tom's powerful performance of the Bond theme is legendary.

5. **a)** *Reload* – This album featured collaborations with contemporary artists and was a massive success.

6. **c)** *The Voice UK* – Tom was a beloved coach on this popular talent show.

7. **b) Wales** – Tom was born and raised in the valleys of

Pontypridd, Wales.

8. **d) Mousse T** – The funky hit "Sex Bomb" was produced by Mousse T.

9. **a) "You Can Leave Your Hat On"** – A memorable moment from his TV show days.

10. **b) "I'll Never Fall in Love Again"** – Tom dedicated this song to his late wife, Linda.

11. **a) 16** – Tom was just a teenager when he became a father.

12. **b) The Cardigans** – They joined forces with Tom for the song "Burning Down the House."

13. **b) Linda** – Tom's beloved wife, who he was devoted to throughout their marriage.

14. **c) 1968** – "Delilah" became one of Tom's signature hits that year.

15. **a) Country song** – The original version of "Green, Green Grass of Home" was a country classic.

16. **b) Elvis Presley** – The King of Rock 'n' Roll was a fan and friend of Tom.

17. **a) 1960s** – Tom's legendary Las Vegas residency began in the late 1960s.

18. **a) *The Simpsons*** – Tom appeared on the show, singing alongside Marge.

19. **a) "It's Not Unusual"** – He performed this classic hit at the Jubilee.

20. **b) "Sex Bomb"** – Those unforgettable lyrics are from this dancefloor anthem.

Scorecard:

- **16–20 Correct:** You're a certified Tom Jones superfan! Sir Tom himself would be proud.
- **11–15 Correct:** Pretty impressive! You definitely know your Tom trivia.
- **6–10 Correct:** Not bad, but time to revisit those classic hits!
- **0–5 Correct:** Don't worry, "It's Not Unusual" to need a refresher. Pop on some Tom Jones and try again!

How did you do? No matter your score, we hope you had fun! Keep dancing, singing, and celebrating the incredible legacy of Sir Tom Jones.

8

Which Tom Jones Song Are You?
Personality Quiz

Are you ready to discover which Tom Jones classic best reflects your personality? From romantic ballads to fiery anthems, Tom's music covers every emotion. This fun personality quiz will help you find out which iconic song captures your essence. Answer each question, tally up your results, and see which Tom Jones song speaks to your soul. Plus, you'll get song recommendations based on your result, so you can keep grooving in true Tom Jones style!

The Quiz

1. **What's your ideal Saturday night?**

- a) Dancing at a lively party with friends
- b) Having a quiet, romantic dinner with someone special
- c) Listening to live music at a cozy venue

- d) Going on an adventure to try something new

1. **How would your friends describe you?**

- a) Passionate and bold
- b) Loyal and loving
- c) Fun-loving and playful
- d) Mysterious and intense

1. **What's your favorite type of movie?**

- a) Romantic drama
- b) Action-packed thriller
- c) Comedy or rom-com
- d) Mystery or crime

1. **What's your go-to outfit?**

- a) Something daring and attention-grabbing
- b) A classic, timeless ensemble
- c) Colorful and a bit quirky
- d) Dark and sophisticated

1. **Which activity sounds the most enjoyable?**

- a) Writing a love letter or expressing your feelings openly
- b) Spending quality time with family or close friends
- c) Going to a comedy show or singing karaoke
- d) Solving a mystery or exploring a new city

1. **How do you handle conflict?**

- a) You approach it head-on, with intense emotion
- b) You try to resolve things calmly and fairly
- c) You use humor to diffuse the tension
- d) You keep things to yourself, revealing only what you want to

1. **What's your dream travel destination?**

- a) Paris – the city of love
- b) Tuscany – warm, scenic, and classic
- c) Las Vegas – lively and entertaining
- d) Scotland – mysterious and full of history

1. **How would you describe your ideal relationship?**

- a) Passionate and intense
- b) Steady, loyal, and supportive
- c) Lighthearted, with lots of laughs
- d) Deep and a little unpredictable

Results: Which Tom Jones Song Are You?

Mostly A's: "Delilah"

You are passionate, fiery, and unafraid to feel things deeply. Like Tom's hit "Delilah," you love intensely and believe in embracing every emotion, from joy to heartbreak. People are drawn to your boldness and your ability to make every moment memorable.

- **Song Recommendation**: Besides "Delilah," check out "Without Love" for more of Tom's intense, emotional songs.

Mostly B's: "Green, Green Grass of Home"

You value loyalty, stability, and the simple pleasures of life. Just like "Green, Green Grass of Home," you find comfort in tradition, family, and familiar places. You're the type who treasures old friendships, keeps promises, and knows the value of a quiet night at home.

- **Song Recommendation**: You'll love "I'll Never Fall in Love Again" for its nostalgic, heartwarming vibes.

Mostly C's: "It's Not Unusual"

You're fun-loving, playful, and full of life! Just like Tom's iconic "It's Not Unusual," you know how to light up a room and make people smile. Your friends know you're the one to call for a good time, and your energy is absolutely infectious.

- **Song Recommendation**: Add "She's a Lady" to your playlist for another upbeat, feel-good Tom Jones classic.

Mostly D's: "Thunderball"

Mysterious, intense, and a bit of a thrill-seeker, you embody the essence of "Thunderball." People are captivated by your depth and the way you carry yourself with quiet confidence. You love a good mystery and are never afraid to venture into the unknown.

- **Song Recommendation**: Dive into "Help Yourself" for

another song that channels your powerful, enigmatic side.

9

Fashion & Style Evolution – The Iconic Looks of a Legend

When it comes to Tom Jones, it's not just his powerful voice and unforgettable songs that have made him a legend—it's also his impeccable sense of style. Whether he's rocking a tailored suit or letting it all hang out with an unbuttoned shirt, Tom has always known how to dress to impress. Over the decades, he's embraced everything from Mod styles to the glitz of Vegas, proving that when it comes to fashion, he's truly "The One."

Let's take a walk through the decades and explore how Tom Jones' fashion choices not only kept him looking sharp but also played a crucial role in establishing his status as a charismatic sex symbol and timeless icon.

Dressing for Success: The Early Years

The Mod Look of the 1960s: Tailored Suits and Classic Pompadour

In the swinging '60s, Tom Jones burst onto the scene with a voice that could melt hearts—and a look to match. From the very beginning, Tom understood that image was everything. In those early years, he embraced the Mod fashion that was sweeping through London, with impeccably tailored suits, crisp white shirts, and slim ties. He kept his hair perfectly coiffed in a stylish pompadour that would make Elvis himself jealous.

Tom's early look was clean, sharp, and sophisticated, reflecting the fashionable London scene that was all about sleek lines and bold statements. The tailored suits helped him project an image of confidence and charisma, which, paired with his soulful voice, made women swoon and men take notes. Let's just say, Tom was "It's Not Unusual" personified—cool, confident, and completely captivating.

The Influence of Mod and Swinging Sixties Fashion on His Style

During the '60s, London was the epicenter of fashion, and Tom Jones was at the heart of it all. Inspired by fashion icons like The Beatles and The Rolling Stones, Tom infused his wardrobe with the same sense of youthful rebellion and stylish elegance. Whether he was performing on *Top of the Pops* or crooning on *The Ed Sullivan Show*, Tom's fashion choices played a huge role in setting him apart from other artists. He was sexy without being over-the-top, classic yet completely unforgettable—a style that would define him for years to come.

The Role of Fashion in Establishing His Image as a Charismatic Sex Symbol

Tom's wardrobe was more than just clothes; it was a statement. In those early years, his sharp suits and smooth dance moves helped cement his status as a sex symbol. With each performance, he became known not just for his voice, but for the way he looked and moved. Let's face it: when Tom Jones shook those hips, it didn't matter what he was wearing—though a well-tailored suit certainly didn't hurt!

The Bold & The Daring: The Glamorous '70s & Vegas Era

The Extravagant Stage Outfits: Sequined Jackets, Velvet Suits, and Flamboyant Shirts

As Tom's career soared, so did his fashion choices. The 1970s were all about excess, and Tom embraced it wholeheartedly. This was the era of his famous Las Vegas residency, where the brighter, shinier, and bolder, the better. Picture this: sequined jackets that sparkled under the neon lights, deep velvet suits in rich jewel tones, and shirts unbuttoned to reveal a glimpse (or more) of his famous chest hair.

The transformation wasn't just about looking good—it was about embracing the larger-than-life persona that Tom had become. Las Vegas was his playground, and he dressed the part. The man who sang "Delilah" in a slick suit now turned heads with gold chains, medallions, and flamboyant shirts that screamed, "I'm here, and I'm fabulous." Tom's style during this period was synonymous with the glamour and excess of the Vegas scene, and fans couldn't get enough of it.

The Iconic Gold Chains, Medallions, and Open-Chested Shirts

Let's talk about those legendary gold chains for a moment. In the '70s, Tom Jones made the bold move of embracing a more casual, sexy look that showcased his masculinity. With his shirts unbuttoned to the navel and a glint of gold around his neck, Tom became the epitome of '70s cool. It was a look that countless men tried to copy, but only Tom could truly pull off. After all, not everyone can turn a simple shirt into a symbol of sex appeal.

Reflecting the Glamour of His Las Vegas Residency

Tom's Vegas residency wasn't just a career milestone; it was a fashion revolution. His extravagant outfits became just as iconic as his hits, turning every performance into a spectacle. Fans came not just for the music but for the chance to see what dazzling ensemble Tom would be wearing next. He was no longer just a singer—he was a fashion icon.

73

Reinvention & Timeless Style

The 1980s & 1990s: From Disco to Classic Elegance

The '80s brought a new era, and Tom was ready for it. As the music world shifted away from disco and toward a more rock-oriented sound, Tom also adapted his style. Gone were the sequins and medallions; in their place came leather jackets, sleek blazers, and classic suits that hinted at a more mature, refined Tom Jones.

During this period, Tom wasn't just a pop star—he was a style icon who knew how to evolve without losing his essence. He embraced leather and denim for a rock 'n' roll edge while still staying true to his roots with tailored suits and crisp shirts. The 1990s saw Tom making a comeback with *Reload*, an album that brought him back into the limelight with a mix of classic elegance and a modern twist.

The 2000s & Beyond: The Gentleman Rocker

As Tom entered the 2000s, he showed the world that style only gets better with age. Gone were the flashy outfits of the '70s, replaced with a more timeless, sophisticated look. Tom embraced monochrome suits, clean lines, and a minimalist aesthetic that still had just enough flair to remind everyone who they were dealing with.

Tom's style became synonymous with the "gentleman rocker" look: a perfect blend of classic elegance and subtle edge. He wasn't just dressing to impress anymore—he was dressing to *express*. Whether it was a sleek black suit or a perfectly fitted leather jacket, Tom's outfits reflected his enduring passion for music and performance.

Collaborations with Fashion Designers and Stylists

To stay relevant in the ever-changing world of fashion, Tom teamed up with designers and stylists who helped him refine his look while keeping it fresh. Collaborations with brands like Paul Smith and tailoring from Savile Row ensured that Tom's wardrobe was as timeless as his voice. He wasn't just following trends—he was setting them.

Maintaining a Signature Style While Staying Current

The secret to Tom's fashion success is simple: he knows how to adapt without losing himself. Even as he embraces new trends, he always stays true to the core elements that define his style. Whether he's performing on stage, appearing on *The Voice UK*, or simply stepping out for an event, Tom's fashion choices are always on point, proving that style, much like his music, is timeless.

Tom Jones: The Man, The Style, The Legend

From the sharp suits of the '60s to the sequined glamour of Vegas and the refined elegance of his later years, Tom Jones has proven time and again that fashion is about more than just clothes—it's about attitude. He's a man who's never been afraid to take risks, both musically and sartorially, and that's why we love him.

So the next time you hear one of his hits, picture Tom in one of his iconic outfits. Because whether he's singing "It's Not Unusual" or "Sex Bomb," one thing is certain: he's going to look *fabulous* doing it.

10

Fashion Icon to Cultural Phenomenon

When it comes to fashion, Tom Jones is much more than just a man in a suit—he's a style icon whose influence has spanned decades. From his daring outfits in the '70s to his timeless elegance today, Tom's sartorial choices have inspired countless artists, performers, and fans. Let's take a look at how Tom's bold fashion sense has left a lasting mark on pop culture and continues to inspire style icons across the world.

Influence on Pop Culture & Style Icons

1. Tom's Bold Fashion as a Statement of Confidence

Tom Jones has always been a master of combining classic style with bold choices that push the envelope. Whether it was the unbuttoned shirts, gold medallions, or velvet blazers, Tom's style was a reflection of his confidence and charisma. It wasn't just about what he wore—it was about how he wore it. He showed the world that fashion could be fun, sexy, and fearless.

2. Inspiring a Generation of Artists and Performers

Tom's influence on fashion isn't limited to the fans who've mimicked his looks over the years. His daring wardrobe choices have inspired a new generation of artists and performers. Stars like Bruno Mars, Harry Styles, and even Lady Gaga have been seen embracing elements of Tom's flamboyant stage style— whether it's Harry Styles rocking a velvet suit or Bruno Mars donning a gold chain reminiscent of Tom's Vegas days.

3. Reflections from Fashion Critics on Tom's Impact

Fashion critics have often praised Tom's ability to adapt to changing trends while staying true to his signature style. According to legendary fashion editor Grace Coddington, "Tom Jones is a rare example of someone who never followed the fashion rules—he made his own." Fashion journalist Suzy Menkes once noted that Tom's use of sequins and velvet in the 1970s set a new standard for stage fashion, influencing everyone from David Bowie to Prince.

4. Fan Tributes: Recreating the Iconic Tom Jones Look

Tom's fashion legacy is kept alive by fans who pay tribute to his iconic looks through cosplay, fan art, and even themed events. At concerts and tribute nights, you'll see fans decked out in Tom's signature outfits—from the sequined jackets and open-chested shirts of his Vegas days to his more recent sleek, monochrome suits. Social media platforms are filled with fan illustrations and photos of fans recreating their favorite Tom looks, proving that his influence is as strong as ever.

Dress Like Tom – A Fashion Guide for Fans

If you've ever watched Tom Jones perform and thought, "I wish I could pull off that look," well, you're in luck! This chapter is all about how you can bring a bit of Tom's iconic style into your own wardrobe. Whether you're aiming for classic elegance, a touch of rock 'n' roll flair, or a full-blown Vegas showman look, we've got you covered. Let's break down how to dress like the legend himself.

Style Tips Inspired by Tom Jones' Wardrobe

1. The Classic Suit and Tie Combo: Channeling 1960s Tom

- For men: Invest in a well-tailored suit in classic colors like black, navy, or charcoal. Pair it with a crisp white shirt and a slim tie. Don't forget the finishing touch—a polished pair of leather shoes.
- For women: A fitted blazer over tailored trousers or a pencil skirt can capture the essence of Tom's sophisticated early look. Add a pair of pointed-toe heels for that extra flair.

2. Going Bold with Velvet and Sequins: The Vegas Look

- For men: To channel Tom's glamorous '70s era, go for a velvet jacket in rich colors like burgundy or emerald green. Add a touch of sparkle with a sequined shirt or accessories. And, of course, don't be afraid to leave a few buttons undone!
- For women: A sequined dress or velvet jumpsuit can capture that bold, show-stopping look. Pair it with statement jewelry and a pair of platform heels to complete the ensemble.

3. The Gentleman Rocker: Modern Monochrome Elegance

- For men: Embrace the sleek, timeless style Tom has perfected in his later years with monochrome outfits. Think black-on-black suits, minimalist leather jackets, and tailored shirts. Keep the accessories simple—a silver watch or understated cufflinks will do the trick.
- For women: A fitted black dress or a sleek pantsuit can achieve that modern, sophisticated look. Pair with minimal jewelry, like hoop earrings or a delicate chain necklace, to keep the focus on the outfit.

Accessorizing Like Tom: The Details That Make the Difference

1. The Perfect Belt Buckle

One of Tom's signature accessories is his bold belt buckle. Opt for a statement belt with a large buckle to add a bit of flair to your outfit. It's a subtle way to nod to Tom's style without going over the top.

2. The Iconic Gold Chain

Tom's gold chains became a staple of his wardrobe during the '70s. If you're feeling bold, wear a chunky gold chain over an unbuttoned shirt for that classic "Sex Bomb" look. For women, a layered gold necklace can add a touch of glam to any outfit.

3. Statement Rings and Cufflinks

Tom knows how to accessorize with class. Whether it's a bold ring or a pair of elegant cufflinks, adding a bit of shine can elevate even the simplest outfit. For women, consider a cocktail ring or statement earrings to channel Tom's love of flashy yet sophisticated accessories.

How to Recreate Tom's Iconic Stage Outfits for Themed Parties or Events

1. The "It's Not Unusual" Classic Look

Perfect for a throwback party, channel Tom's early days with a fitted suit, a crisp shirt, and polished shoes. Add a skinny tie and slick back your hair to complete the look. For women, a tailored blazer and pencil skirt combo will have you looking sharp and stylish.

2. The Vegas Showman

If you're attending a themed party or just want to go all out, embrace Tom's Vegas style. Think sequins, velvet, and as much bling as you can manage. For men, don a sequined blazer and leave your shirt unbuttoned For women, a sparkly mini dress with platform heels will turn heads.

3. The Modern Gentleman Rocker

For a more subtle yet sophisticated look, go for a monochrome outfit with clean lines. Men can opt for a black leather jacket over a fitted shirt, while women can wear a sleek black dress with ankle boots. Keep accessories minimal to maintain that effortless, cool vibe.

Embracing Tom's Timeless Style: The Takeaway

At the end of the day, Tom Jones' fashion isn't just about clothes—it's about attitude. Whether you're dressing up for a themed event or just want to add a touch of Tom's swagger to your everyday look, the key is to wear it with confidence. Tom's style evolved over the decades, but he always stayed true to himself. So, whatever look you're going for, remember the most important accessory: confidence.

So go ahead—put on your best outfit, throw on some Tom Jones hits, and dance like no one's watching. After all, as Sir Tom has shown us time and again, fashion is all about having fun and expressing yourself.

11

Collaborations – A Journey Through Decades of Musical Partnerships

The Art of Collaboration

Tom Jones has always been a man of many talents, but one of his greatest strengths is his ability to collaborate with other artists. Whether it's trading soulful verses with a rock legend or blending his deep baritone with the smooth vocals of a pop star, Tom knows how to bring out the best in a partnership. But it's not just about the music—Tom's collaborative spirit has been key to keeping his sound fresh, relevant, and timeless.

So, what's his secret? It's simple: Tom has always embraced change and innovation, proving that you're never too old to learn something new. His willingness to step outside his comfort zone and work with artists from different genres has not only kept him at the forefront of the music industry but also allowed him to continually reinvent himself. This chapter is a celebration of Tom's incredible journey through decades of collaborations that helped shape his career into what it is today.

The Early Years: Duets & Cross-Genre Pairings

The 1960s: The Magic of *This Is Tom Jones*

In the late 1960s, Tom Jones became a household name thanks to his hit TV show *This Is Tom Jones.* But it wasn't just Tom's powerful voice and charismatic presence that captivated audiences—it was his ability to seamlessly blend with other musical legends. Every week, viewers tuned in to see Tom sharing the stage with the likes of Janis Joplin, Aretha Franklin, and Dusty Springfield.

Who can forget the electrifying duet with Janis Joplin? Their rendition of "Raise Your Hand" was a thrilling mix of rock and soul that left fans breathless. Tom's chemistry with Aretha Franklin was equally unforgettable, as the two traded powerful vocals that brought the house down. These collaborations weren't just entertaining—they showcased Tom's versatility, proving he could keep up with the best in any genre.

The 1970s: Country Crossovers and Vegas Glamour

As Tom's star continued to rise in the 1970s, he expanded his collaborative efforts beyond pop and rock. He teamed up with country legends like Tammy Wynette and Johnny Cash, proving that his rich, soulful voice could shine in any musical setting. One particularly memorable performance was his duet with

Johnny Cash on "I Walk the Line," blending their distinctive vocal styles into a harmonious masterpiece.

During his iconic Las Vegas residency, Tom shared the stage with some of the biggest names in show business, including Elvis Presley and Sammy Davis Jr. The camaraderie between Tom and Elvis was palpable; they often joked around backstage and even performed impromptu duets after hours. Tom's collaborations during this period helped cement his reputation as one of the most versatile performers of his time, capable of captivating audiences in any setting.

How These Early Collaborations Shaped Tom's Legacy

These early collaborations were more than just great performances — they were pivotal in establishing Tom's reputation as a charismatic and versatile artist. By stepping outside his comfort zone and exploring new genres, Tom built a career that wasn't limited to just pop hits. He became a true entertainer who could connect with audiences across genres and generations.

The Reinvention of the '90s: The Reload Era

The Story Behind the *Reload* Album (1999)

By the late 1990s, Tom was ready for a fresh challenge. Enter *Reload*, the album that would redefine his career and introduce him to a whole new audience. *Reload* was a collection of covers, but with a twist — each track was a collaboration with contemporary artists. The album featured an eclectic mix of musicians, from indie rock bands to pop stars, each bringing their own unique flavor to Tom's timeless voice.

Collaborations with Contemporary Artists

One of the standout tracks was "Burning Down the House," where Tom teamed up with The Cardigans. Their playful rendition of the Talking Heads classic became an instant hit, breathing new life into the song and earning Tom praise from a younger generation of fans. Then there was the unforgettable duet with the Stereophonics on "Mama Told Me Not to Come," which blended rock and soul in a way that only Tom could pull off. Robbie Williams also joined the fun with "Are You Gonna Go My Way," bringing his cheeky energy to match Tom's.

The Unexpected Success of *Reload*

Reload was more than just a comeback—it became one of Tom's best-selling albums, proving that his appeal was truly ageless. The album topped the charts, sold millions of copies, and introduced Tom to a whole new generation who were just discovering his music. It was a testament to his ability to adapt, evolve, and stay relevant even after decades in the business.

How Tom's Willingness to Collaborate with Younger Artists Kept Him Relevant

Tom's willingness to work with younger musicians not only expanded his fan base but also showed that he was never content to rest on his laurels. By embracing new sounds and styles, Tom proved that great music transcends age, genre, and time. It was the perfect example of how collaboration can breathe new life into a career and keep it going strong.

Experimenting with Different Genres: Hip-Hop, R&B, and Dance

"Sex Bomb" with Wyclef Jean: A Dance Floor Sensation

If there's one song that proved Tom could still dominate the dance charts, it was "Sex Bomb." Produced by Wyclef Jean, the track became a global hit, filling dance floors from London to New York. With its funky beat, cheeky lyrics, and Tom's sultry delivery, "Sex Bomb" showed that the Welsh crooner could groove just as hard as any modern pop star.

Soulful Collaborations with Jools Holland's Rhythm & Blues Orchestra

Tom also delved into R&B and soul, collaborating with Jools Holland and his Rhythm & Blues Orchestra. Tracks like "It'll Be Me" and "St. James Infirmary Blues" highlighted Tom's deep connection to blues and jazz, genres that had always been close to his heart. These collaborations allowed him to revisit his musical roots while also exploring new directions.

Exploring Electronic and Dance Music with Chicane and Art of Noise

Never one to shy away from experimentation, Tom even ventured into electronic music. His collaboration with Chicane on the track "Stoned in Love" brought him back into the dance charts, while his work with Art of Noise on "Kiss" introduced the Prince classic to a whole new audience. These genre-blending projects proved that Tom could seamlessly transition into any musical style while maintaining his signature sound.

How These Genre-Crossing Collaborations Expanded Tom's Musical Range

From hip-hop to electronic dance music, Tom's willingness to collaborate across genres kept him in the spotlight. By teaming up with artists from different musical worlds, he not only expanded his own repertoire but also showed that his voice could adapt to any style. It's no wonder that, even after more than six decades in the industry, Tom Jones remains as relevant as ever.

The Legacy of Collaboration

Tom Jones' career is a testament to the power of collaboration. From his early duets with legends like Janis Joplin to his modern-day partnerships with pop stars, Tom has always been open to new experiences. It's this willingness to embrace change, take risks, and work with others that has kept his sound fresh and his career thriving.

As Tom continues to perform and collaborate with artists of all ages, it's clear that his journey is far from over. And if there's one thing we've learned, it's that when Tom Jones teams up with another artist, magic happens.

12

The Man, The Mentor, The Legend

As the years go by, many artists fade into the background, but Tom Jones has done just the opposite. With a career spanning over six decades, he continues to surprise, inspire, and delight fans with his music. In recent years, Tom has embraced new collaborations, stripped-down acoustic sessions, and even taken on the role of a mentor. Let's explore how Tom has reinvented himself in the 2000s and beyond, leaving a lasting legacy that proves his talent is truly timeless.

Acoustic, Blues & Intimate Sessions: Returning to His Roots

Collaborations in the 2000s and Beyond

Tom's love for raw, unfiltered music has always been at the heart of his sound, but in the 2000s, he went back to his roots with a series of acoustic and blues projects that showcased his powerful voice in its purest form. Collaborating with artists like

Cerys Matthews, Joss Stone, and Jack White, Tom stripped away the flashy production to focus on the soul of the music.

"Praise & Blame" – The Gospel and Blues Revival

In 2010, Tom released *Praise & Blame*, an album that was a departure from his previous work. It featured gospel and blues influences, with a raw, intimate sound that was both refreshing and unexpected. Tracks like "Burning Hell" and "Did Trouble Me" allowed Tom to explore the deeper, more soulful side of his voice.

These collaborations were a chance for Tom to reconnect with the music that inspired him in his early years. Working with artists like Jack White, who produced his haunting cover of "Evil," brought a gritty edge to Tom's sound, proving that even in his 70s, he was still willing to take creative risks.

How These Projects Demonstrated His Timeless Vocal Power

These acoustic and blues collaborations weren't just about nostalgia—they were about evolution. Tom's voice, seasoned with time, resonated with an emotional depth that only comes from a lifetime of experience. These projects allowed him to showcase his versatility and cemented his reputation as one of the greatest voices of all time.

Mentoring on The Voice UK & Collaborating with New Talent

Becoming a Mentor on *The Voice UK*

In 2012, Tom took on a new role as a coach on *The Voice UK*. Here, he was no longer just a performer but a mentor, guiding young artists on their journey to stardom. His wisdom, warmth, and willingness to share his experiences won the hearts of both contestants and viewers alike. Tom's influence on the show went beyond just coaching—he often performed with the contestants, showing them how to command a stage with confidence and charisma.

Collaborations with Contestants and Emerging Artists

Tom's time on *The Voice UK* wasn't just about mentoring; it was also about collaborating with fresh talent. His performances with contestants brought new life to classic songs. For example, his duet with Leanne Mitchell on "Mama Told Me Not to Come" was a highlight that showcased how Tom could seamlessly blend his voice with newcomers.

Partnering with Modern Artists: Jessie J, Ed Sheeran, and Rag'n'Bone Man

Tom's collaborative spirit didn't stop at *The Voice*. He continued to partner with contemporary artists, bridging the gap between generations. Collaborations with Jessie J on *The Voice*, a surprise performance with Ed Sheeran at the Brit Awards, and a soulful duet with Rag'n'Bone Man on "Georgia on My Mind" proved that Tom was not just a legend from the past but a force to be reckoned with in the present.

How These Collaborations Cemented His Legacy

Tom's willingness to embrace new talent and collaborate with young artists showcased his openness to change and growth. By staying engaged with the next generation, he ensured that his music remained relevant, inspiring fans of all ages. His mentorship has left a lasting impact on the music industry, proving that true legends never stop learning, teaching, and growing.

Fan Favorites: Best Duets & Hidden Gems

A Curated List of Beloved Collaborations

Over the years, Tom Jones has delivered some truly memorable duets. Here's a look at some fan favorites:

1. **"You've Lost That Lovin' Feelin'"** with Dusty Springfield

This classic duet remains one of the most beloved performances from *This Is Tom Jones*.

1. **"Burning Down the House"** with The Cardigans

A high-energy collaboration that brought a modern twist to the Talking Heads' classic.

1. **"Mama Told Me Not to Come"** with Stereophonics

A fun, soulful rendition that brought Tom back into the charts.

1. **"Cry to Me"** with Joss Stone

A sultry, soulful performance that highlighted Tom's ability to connect with younger artists.

1. **"Ain't No Sunshine"** with Beverley Knight

A powerful duet that showcased Tom's timeless voice alongside Beverley's soulful tones.

Behind-the-Scenes Stories

Tom's collaborations are often filled with behind-the-scenes stories that fans adore. For instance, his duet with Janis Joplin was not just a TV moment but a meeting of musical minds backstage, where they bonded over their shared love of blues music. Meanwhile, his surprise performance with Ed Sheeran was put together in just a few days, proving that Tom's spontaneity is still very much alive.

Hidden Gems That Showcase His Versatility

There are countless lesser-known tracks where Tom's collaborative magic shines. For example, his cover of Leonard Cohen's "Tower of Song" on *Spirit in the Room* is a hauntingly beautiful rendition that fans often overlook. Similarly, his duet with Cerys Matthews on "Baby, It's Cold Outside" is a playful, jazzy take that's perfect for holiday playlists.

The Lasting Legacy of Tom Jones' Collaborations

How These Partnerships Have Enriched Tom's Career

Tom Jones' collaborations have done more than just add hits to his discography—they've enriched his career by keeping him connected to new musical trends and generations of fans. His willingness to collaborate has brought him into new musical landscapes, whether it's dance tracks with Wyclef Jean or soulful ballads with Joss Stone.

Bridging Fans Across Generations and Genres

Tom's collaborative spirit has brought together fans from all walks of life. Whether it's a 20-something discovering him through a collaboration with a modern artist or a long-time fan who has followed him since the '60s, Tom's music has a way of bringing people together. His ability to bridge musical worlds proves that great music transcends time, trends, and generations.

Celebrating Tom's Unique Ability to Bridge Musical Worlds

Tom Jones is not just a singer; he's a musical chameleon who's mastered the art of collaboration. Whether he's performing an intimate acoustic set or belting out a dance hit, Tom's ability to connect with other artists and his audience is unparalleled. His collaborations are a testament to his love of music and his belief that great things happen when artists come together.

13

Dance Style – Shaking Things Up

T om Jones isn't just known for that powerful baritone voice; he's also famous for his electrifying dance moves. From his early days in the '60s to his more mature performances in recent years, Tom's dance style has played a crucial role in shaping his persona as a charismatic performer. Let's dive into the origins, signature moves, and the cultural impact of Tom's iconic stage presence. Whether it was a seductive hip thrust or a smooth body roll, Tom's moves have left fans cheering (and occasionally throwing their underwear) for decades.

The Origins of Tom's Dance Style

The Influence of 1960s Pop and Rock 'n' Roll Dance Moves

In the early years of his career, Tom Jones' dance style was heavily influenced by the pop and rock 'n' roll scene of the

1960s. It was an era when performers like Elvis Presley, Jackie Wilson, and James Brown were known for combining music with mesmerizing dance moves. Tom was no exception. From the very beginning, he knew that music was as much about the show as it was about the sound.

Inspirations from Elvis Presley and Jackie Wilson

Elvis Presley, the King of Rock 'n' Roll, was undoubtedly a major influence on Tom's stage persona. Tom admired how Elvis could captivate an audience with just a swivel of his hips. Another key influence was Jackie Wilson, known for his dynamic performances and acrobatic moves. Tom took inspiration from both but added his own twist, infusing these classic moves with his unique, raw energy.

How Jones Infused Traditional Dance Moves with His Own Flair

While Tom borrowed from the best, he made the moves his own. His dance style was all about spontaneity, driven by the music and the energy of the crowd. Tom's distinctive flair came from blending the smooth moves of his influences with a bold, confident attitude. His movements were expressive, sexy, and sometimes cheeky, reflecting his onstage persona as a fearless entertainer who wasn't afraid to turn up the heat.

Signature Dance Moves Breakdown

A. "The Hip Thrust"

Let's start with the most iconic move in Tom Jones' repertoire: the hip thrust. Fans who attended his concerts or watched him on TV couldn't get enough of this signature move. The combination of his deep, sultry voice with those rhythmic hip thrusts was enough to send fans into a frenzy. Whether he was performing "It's Not Unusual" or "Sex Bomb," Tom's hip thrusts became a staple of his sensual performance style.

- **Famous Performances**: His performance of "It's Not Unusual" on *Top of the Pops* and countless live shows where fans would scream (and occasionally faint) every time he moved those hips.
- **Why It Worked**: The hip thrust wasn't just a dance move; it was a statement. It exuded confidence, playfulness, and a touch of cheekiness that made Tom's performances unforgettable.

B. "The Microphone Stand Swing"

Another signature move in Tom's arsenal was the way he used his microphone stand. Rather than letting it sit idly, Tom would grab it, swing it around, and use it as a prop in his choreography. The mic stand became an extension of his performance, adding drama and flair to his songs.

- **Examples**: During live performances of "Delilah," Tom would swing the mic stand in time with the music, emphasizing key moments in the song.

- **Why It Worked**: The microphone stand swing added a sense of theatricality, turning each performance into a visual spectacle.

C. "The Hand Gestures and Pointing"

Tom's expressive hand movements were another signature element of his stage presence. Whether he was pointing directly at a fan in the audience or gesturing to emphasize a lyric, his hand movements added an extra layer of drama to his performances.

- **Songs like "Delilah"** featured confident pointing gestures that made the audience feel like Tom was singing directly to them.
- **Why It Worked**: These gestures were a way for Tom to connect with his audience, making each performance feel personal and engaging.

D. "The Footwork and Leg Kicks"

Tom's performances were full of energy, and his footwork was no exception. From quick shuffles to high leg kicks, Tom's agile moves kept the energy high, especially during upbeat songs like "What's New Pussycat?"

- **Evolution**: While his earlier performances featured more energetic leg kicks and fast footwork, as Tom aged, he transitioned to more subtle, yet still charismatic, movements.
- **Why It Worked**: The dynamic footwork added excitement

and rhythm to his performances, showing that Tom was a true entertainer from head to toe.

E. "The Swaying and Body Rolls"

Not every song required high-energy moves. For his ballads, Tom would slow things down with smooth, rhythmic swaying and body rolls that added a sensual touch. Songs like "Green, Green Grass of Home" showcased his ability to convey deep emotion through simple, fluid movements.

- **Why It Worked**: The body rolls were all about control and finesse, matching the mood of slower, more soulful songs and showing that Tom could be both powerful and gentle.

The Role of Dance in Building His Persona

Tom Jones' dance moves weren't just for show—they were a reflection of his confident, bold personality. Each move was an extension of who he was: a charismatic, fearless performer who knew how to work a crowd. His dance style helped cement his reputation as a sex symbol, with fans throwing lingerie on stage as a testament to his magnetic presence.

Tom's physicality enhanced his live performances, making them memorable experiences that audiences would talk about for years. His moves weren't just choreography; they were part of what made Tom Jones, well, Tom Jones.

Fan Reactions and Cultural Impact

Tom's dance moves didn't just influence fans—they became a part of pop culture. The frenzy he created on stage led to countless parodies and tributes in TV shows and movies. His hip thrusts and mic stand swings became iconic enough to be imitated by everyone from comedians to fellow musicians.

Other performers have taken inspiration from Tom's stage presence, proving that his influence reaches far beyond his own performances. Artists like Mick Jagger, Robbie Williams, and even Justin Timberlake have cited Tom's ability to command a stage as inspiration for their own dance styles.

Evolution of His Dance Moves Over the Decades

Early Energetic Performances vs. Later Refined Moves

In his younger years, Tom's performances were all about energy—high kicks, fast footwork, and explosive hip thrusts. As he grew older, Tom adapted his style to suit his age, focusing on more refined movements that still carried the same charisma.

How He Adapted While Retaining His Signature Flair

Even in his later years, Tom's performances remained captivating. He transitioned from high-energy moves to smoother, more soulful gestures, showing that while he might slow down, his passion never would. His evolution is a testament to his ability to adapt while staying true to himself.

Conclusion: The Timelessness of Tom Jones' Dance Moves

Tom Jones' dance style is more than just a collection of moves—it's a testament to his unparalleled showmanship. Whether it's the seductive hip thrusts or the expressive hand gestures, Tom's moves have stood the test of time. His dance style remains iconic, proving that when it comes to entertaining a crowd, it's all about confidence, passion, and a little bit of flair.

Tom's dance moves are as timeless as his voice, and they continue to inspire performers and delight fans. So, the next time you find yourself dancing along to "It's Not Unusual," remember—you're carrying on the legacy of one of the greatest showmen of all time.

14

Greatest Hits & Discography – A Guide to the Music of a Legend

Tom Jones' music catalog is as rich and diverse as his career, spanning genres from pop to blues, gospel to dance. With decades of unforgettable hits, he's captured the hearts of fans around the world. But beyond his chart-toppers, Tom's discography includes hidden gems that showcase his artistry in ways mainstream listeners might have missed. This chapter is a journey through the essential tracks, albums, and underrated cuts that every Tom Jones fan should know.

Essential Tom Jones Playlist

Whether you're new to Tom Jones or a longtime fan looking for a playlist that covers his most iconic songs, this collection brings together the best of his music. Here are the top tracks that define his career, capturing the unique power of his voice and his boundless charisma.

1. **"It's Not Unusual" (1965)**

The song that started it all, "It's Not Unusual" remains one of Tom's most beloved hits. With its upbeat brass, catchy melody, and, of course, those iconic hip swings, this track is a must-listen for any fan.

1. **"What's New Pussycat?" (1965)**

Written by Burt Bacharach and Hal David, this playful, quirky tune has become synonymous with Tom's charm. Its catchy chorus is unforgettable and pure fun.

1. **"Delilah" (1968)**

A passionate anthem of heartbreak and betrayal, "Delilah" showcases Tom's storytelling ability and vocal power. It's a dramatic, emotional rollercoaster that never loses its appeal.

1. **"Green, Green Grass of Home" (1967)**

This nostalgic ballad about home and longing struck a chord with audiences and remains one of Tom's most moving songs.

1. **"She's a Lady" (1971)**

Written by Paul Anka, "She's a Lady" became a defining song of Tom's career. Its groovy, upbeat feel captures his smooth style and charisma.

1. **"I'll Never Fall in Love Again" (1967)**

A soulful, bittersweet ballad that perfectly captures the pain and beauty of love. It's a track that showcases Tom's emotional range.

1. **"Thunderball" (1965)**

The theme song for the James Bond movie of the same name, "Thunderball" is dramatic, intense, and perfectly suited to Tom's powerful voice.

1. **"Sex Bomb" (1999)**

This late-career dance hit with Wyclef Jean gave Tom a whole new audience and became an anthem on the dance floor. It's cheeky, fun, and undeniably catchy.

1. **"Help Yourself" (1968)**

A joyful, upbeat song with a touch of Italian flavor that became one of Tom's biggest hits in Europe. Its infectious energy makes it a fan favorite.

1. **"Burning Down the House" (with The Cardigans) (1999)**

A standout track from his *Reload* album, this Talking Heads cover shows Tom's ability to adapt to new genres and appeal to younger listeners.

1. **"Mama Told Me Not to Come" (with Stereophonics)**

(1999)

Another hit from *Reload*, this collaboration with Stereophonics gave a bluesy, rock edge to the Randy Newman classic, showcasing Tom's versatility.

1. **"Kiss" (with Art of Noise) (1988)**

Tom's funky cover of Prince's "Kiss" brought a fresh twist to the song and became a hit on both sides of the Atlantic.

Essential Albums Overview:

- **Along Came Jones** (1965) – Tom's debut album featuring "It's Not Unusual" and a collection of covers that introduced his voice to the world.
- **Green, Green Grass of Home** (1967) – Known for its title track, this album solidified Tom's reputation for soulful ballads.
- **Tom** (1970) – Featuring "I'll Never Fall in Love Again" and "Daughter of Darkness," this album explored deeper, soulful sounds.
- **Reload** (1999) – This album marked a career renaissance, packed with collaborations and modern covers that reintroduced Tom to a new generation.
- **Praise & Blame** (2010) – A return to his gospel and blues roots, this stripped-down album showed a raw, intimate side of Tom.

Hidden Gems & B-Sides

For dedicated fans, there's a wealth of underrated tracks in Tom's catalog that reveal different facets of his talent. These hidden gems range from deep cuts to lesser-known singles, and each is a testament to Tom's ability to experiment and evolve.

1. **"I (Who Have Nothing)" (1970)**

A powerful, soulful track that brings out the raw emotion in Tom's voice. Though not as popular as his other hits, it's a must-hear for fans of his ballads.

1. **"Evil" (Produced by Jack White) (2012)**

A gritty, bluesy track that Jack White produced for Tom's *Spirit in the Room* album. It's a darker, edgier side of Tom that's both haunting and captivating.

1. **"Resurrection Shuffle" (1971)**

This funky, upbeat track showcases Tom's rock side and highlights his ability to bring energy and life to every performance.

1. **"If I Only Knew" (1994)**

A funky, groove-filled track that introduced Tom to the dance floor. It's a song that's easy to miss but shows off Tom's adaptability.

1. **"Dimming of the Day" (2012)**

A stunningly beautiful cover of Richard Thompson's song from *Spirit in the Room*. It's soft, introspective, and reveals Tom's tender side.

1. **"Promise Her Anything" (1966)**

A fun, playful track that Tom recorded for the soundtrack of the same name. It's a little-known gem that captures the charm of his early work.

1. **"Did Trouble Me" (2010)**

From *Praise & Blame*, this gospel-inspired track has a raw, stripped-back feel. It's a spiritual, emotional performance that shows Tom's powerful connection to blues and gospel.

1. **"Stoned in Love" (with Chicane) (2006)**

A collaboration with electronic producer Chicane, this track took Tom into electronic dance music and became a hit in the UK. It's a unique blend of styles that shows his versatility.

1. **"He Was a Friend of Mine" (2002)**

This song from *Mr. Jones* offers a raw, emotional tribute to a lost friend, showcasing Tom's heartfelt storytelling.

1. **"Somethin' 'Bout You Baby I Like" (1974)**

A fun, catchy tune with a country-pop twist that's often over-looked. It's upbeat and charming, perfect for fans looking to explore Tom's lesser-known work.

Additional Album Highlights:

- **Spirit in the Room** (2012) – A reflective, bluesy album featuring covers of Leonard Cohen, Paul McCartney, and Paul Simon songs. It's intimate and introspective, a must-listen for fans seeking something soulful.
- **The Lead and How to Swing It** (1994) – A 90s experiment that blends rock, pop, and electronic elements. It's a hidden gem that showcases Tom's fearless approach to genre-blending.
- **Mr. Jones** (2002) – An album that flew under the radar but includes some of Tom's most introspective tracks. It's an emotional journey worth exploring.

Conclusion: A Musical Legacy Worth Exploring

Whether it's the iconic hits that define his career or the hidden gems that reveal his artistic depth, Tom Jones' discography is a journey through decades of musical evolution. This curated guide to his music celebrates both the classics and the tracks that deserve more attention, capturing the essence of a performer who's always stayed true to his voice while embracing new sounds. Enjoy the playlist and let yourself be swept away by the unmistakable sound of Sir Tom Jones!

15

Celebrating the Timeless Legacy of Tom Jones

Reflecting on the remarkable career of Tom Jones, it becomes clear that his influence on the music industry is truly enduring. Few artists have been able to captivate generations with the same unwavering energy and charisma that he has brought to his music. From his early days in the swinging 1960s, when he first grabbed the world's attention with that unmistakable baritone and magnetic stage presence, to his more recent collaborations that prove he is as innovative as ever, Tom Jones has created a legacy that's timeless and universal.

Tom's career spans more than six decades, yet his impact remains as strong as ever. His voice has been a constant—rich, powerful, and able to evoke both joy and heartache in equal measure. His music defies simple categorization; it's soulful, intense, playful, and powerful all at once. Whether it's the dramatic build of "Delilah," the joyful energy of "It's Not Unusual," or the raw power of his blues-inspired albums, each song is a reflection of Tom's talent and versatility. He's a musical chameleon, able to shift seamlessly from pop to soul, rock to gospel, and everything in between, all while staying true to himself. And that's precisely what makes his legacy so powerful: his ability to evolve while maintaining an identity that is uniquely his own.

In the '60s and '70s, Tom Jones quickly established himself as a heartthrob and a pop icon, but he never settled for just one label. He wasn't satisfied with being known only as a pop singer, nor was he afraid to take risks, experimenting with new styles and sounds that would keep his music fresh and relevant. He made music that defined eras and moments, yet he never became trapped in them. His career journey has always been forward-looking, seeking out new challenges and collaborations that showcase his timeless voice. Tom's adaptability has kept him at the forefront of popular music for over half a century, proving that true talent knows no boundaries.

Tom's influence on the music industry goes beyond his hit records. He has paved the way for countless artists who look up to him as a model of what it means to be a consummate performer. For musicians, his career offers a master class in longevity, showmanship, and resilience. Tom's willingness to explore different genres and collaborate with a diverse array of artists—from Wyclef Jean and The Cardigans to Jessie J and Jack White—illustrates his openness and his eagerness to learn, even from the next generation of musicians. He's shown that it's possible to grow and adapt without losing the essence of what makes you unique. His willingness to take risks has inspired young artists to be fearless, to push boundaries, and to believe that they too can thrive for decades.

But Tom's music is not just about innovation or industry accolades; it's about connection. His songs have an emotional depth that resonates deeply with listeners. Whether he's singing about heartbreak or joy, there's a raw honesty in his voice that makes his music feel personal. Tom's music isn't just something you listen to—it's something you feel. Each performance is an invitation to experience life's ups and downs, its celebrations and sorrows, right alongside him. His connection with his fans goes beyond the stage and screen; it's deeply emotional and lasting.

Speaking of his fans, no celebration of Tom Jones would be complete without acknowledging the incredible support he has received over the years. Tom has always been open about the gratitude he feels for his fans, the people who have made his career possible. It's his fans who've shown up for concerts, bought records, and requested his songs on the radio for decades, helping him reach new heights and inspiring him to keep going. Tom's fans are known for their enthusiasm, and they're as much a part of his legacy as the music itself. From the early days of throwing flowers (and occasionally underwear!) on stage to today's digital-age fan tributes, they've kept the spirit of his music alive.

Tom's fans are a unique group, spanning generations and crossing borders. They've kept him relevant, passed his music down to their children, and helped introduce his songs to new listeners around the world. They've been there to cheer him on, no matter the stage or the era, whether he was performing on *Top of the Pops* in the '60s, rocking Las Vegas in the '70s, or mentoring young artists on *The Voice UK* in recent years. The bond between Tom and his fans is one of mutual appreciation and respect—a shared understanding that music can bridge generations and bring people together in a way that few other things can.

As we look forward, it's clear that Tom's story is far from over. His voice, his charisma, and his undeniable talent are as potent today as they were when he first began. For those who have grown up with his music, there's a sense of nostalgia that comes with every song, a reminder of moments shared with friends, family, and loved ones. And for new fans just discovering his music, there's an invitation to explore an extensive catalog that spans emotions, styles, and themes, each song as meaningful today as it was when it was recorded.

If Tom's career has taught us anything, it's that music has the power to transcend time. His songs have a timeless quality, speaking to both universal emotions and personal memories. They're woven into the fabric of our lives, marking first dances, first heartbreaks, and late nights spent dancing with friends. Tom's music isn't just a soundtrack—it's a companion to our own journeys, reminding us to be bold, to love deeply, and to live fully. Through his music, he's created a legacy that's both universal and deeply personal, a legacy that each listener can carry forward in their own unique way.

So, as we conclude this celebration of Sir Tom Jones, let's remember that his story is one we all share. Whether you're a lifelong fan or just discovering his music, there's something in

Tom's catalog for everyone. Let's continue to honor his legacy by keeping his music alive, by sharing it with those we love, and by passing it down to future generations. After all, Tom Jones' music is a gift that's meant to be shared, to be enjoyed, and to be celebrated.

In closing, here's to the music, the memories, and the magic of Tom Jones. Here's to the moments that his songs have marked in our lives and the moments yet to come. Let's keep dancing, keep singing, and keep celebrating the incredible journey of one of music's greatest legends. Because as long as there are fans to sing along, the spirit of Tom Jones will never fade.

Printed in Great Britain
by Amazon

59028292R00069